Mugsborough Then and Now: Robert Tressell's 'The Ragged Trousered Philanthropists' Revisited

David E Lowes

2020

First published: February 2020

ISBN: 9798617758872

Table of Contents

Preface iii
Introduction v
Anti-Socialism 1
Apprentices 7
Causes of Poverty 10
Charity 15
Debt 19
Fatalism 23
Foreigners 29
Free Trade 33
Freedom 36
Hire System 39
Homelessness 42
Landlordism 44
Living Wage 48
Machinery 52
Media 56
Money 61
Monopoly 68
Piece-Work 70
Politics 73
Poverty 80
Suicide 85
Unnecessary Work 89
Welfare 93
Conclusion 99
Further Reading 106

Preface

The story of Robert Tressell and his book has been told and re-told by various authors, each account framed in accordance with their own perspective. His novel has also been the subject of academic scrutiny and literary criticism, but the approach adopted here is different. It focuses on the striking, not to say shocking parallels with modern day Britain that were identified and discussed during a course taught under the auspices of Liverpool University's Continuing Education Department in 2019: 'Ragged Trousered Philanthropy: the Political Economy of Robert Tressell.' In part, therefore, the participants are owed a debt of gratitude for their contributions to the insights that follow.

Needless to say, the imperative for completing this work lies in the result of the 2019 General Election.

Introduction

The idea that the attitudes, conditions and experiences described by Robert Tressell still resonate is not a new one. More than 30 years ago, Dave Alfred, the editor of *Robert Tressell Lectures, 1981-88*, made the following comment in his Tribute to Fred Ball: 'Then I read *The Ragged Trousered Philanthropists* and could hardly believe ... that such a book could exist: so direct, so humane and so relevant to today.' Later, in his introduction to the *Lectures* he remarks: 'few can read it and not ask themselves whether it is (still) relevant today' and adds '... is the structure of British society today basically the same as Tressell described it?'

Such sentiments were echoed by Deputy General Secretary of the TUC Norman Willis, in his 1983 lecture: 'too much of what is in Noonan's book still exists.' The following year, Jack Jones, former General Secretary of the Transport and General Workers Union (now Unite) and an activist for pensioners' rights used his lecture to lambast the media, establishment Christians and their contribution to working class ignorance, divisions and subservience. Two years later Tony Benn echoed Jones' sentiments about the press, described the BBC as serving a similar purpose to the Medieval Church, and repeated his derision of the return to Victorian values. He also noted how on repeated occasions 'the working class had to pay the price for the capitalist crisis.'

This last point is particularly pertinent as Tressell's book was written in the aftermath of the 'long depression' that affected Britain, Europe and North America. Britain had also experienced another depression in 1903, a slight improvement from 1905 to 1907 and a full-blown crisis in 1908 – 9. Of course, Benn's talk was given in the wake of the 1973 'oil crisis' and amidst the carnage of de-industrialization - much the same as we are still living with the consequences of the 2008 'financial crash.'

Nevertheless, it seems implausible to suggest that the topics discussed in this book are merely symptoms of economic crisis. Britain in the 1950s, for example, was held to be an affluent society with dramatically rising standards of living and yet *The Poor and the Poorest* (1965), revealed that 7.5 million people were living in relative poverty, with half of those affected in paid employment. The authors also pointed out that thousands of children were being placed in local authority care as a consequence of sub-standard housing.

Attempts were made to redress such shortcomings by means of expanded welfare provision, including the Children and Young Persons Act 1969; the Local Authority Social Services Act 1970; and the Chronically Sick and Disabled Persons Act 1970. Nevertheless, the simple assumption that a growing economy makes extra resources available to provide such services, fails to explain why they were needed in the first place. A similar point can be made about Tax Credits that are designed to supplement the income of people on low wages or, as the title of the Treasury's 2000 report styled it: *Tackling Poverty and Making Work Pay – Tax Credits for the 21st Century.*

The main purpose of what follows is to highlight similarities between Tressell's description of early 20th century Britain and its 21st century counterpart. As the Table of Contents outlines, this is achieved by identifying and illustrating specific areas of analogy. Each chapter is split into two parts entitled 'Tressell' and '21st Century.' The first section quotes examples from *The Ragged Trousered Philanthropists* and in the second part evidence based modern-day equivalents are introduced, albeit without a detailed explanation of how or why they are considered relevant. This is because the intention is to prompt analogies rather than offer analysis or solutions. Nevertheless, many of the areas discussed are interlinked and small capitals are used to indicate areas that overlap and facilitate cross-referencing between chapters.

Discussion of the causes and effects of apparently enduring phenomena is confined to the concluding chapter, so as to avoid the conflation of particular examples with general observations. This addresses five broad themes, in the hope of providing a broader historical perspective,: La Belle Époque & the End of Boom and Bust; From Cradle to Grave - the birth and Death of the Welfare State; The Causes of Poverty &

the Age of Austerity; Fiscal Policy, Tariff Reform & Brexit; and, Killing Machines & the 4th Industrial Revolution.

Anti-Socialism

Tressell

With the exceptions of young Frankie, Nora Owen and the anonymous outriders of the Socialist Van, George Barrington and Frank Owen are the main advocates for socialism as the solution to society's ills. That their task is far from easy, is made clear in the Preface:

> '... not only are the majority of people opposed to Socialism, but a very brief conversation with an average anti-socialist is sufficient to show that he does not know what Socialism means. The same is true of all the anti-socialist writers and the 'great statesmen' who make anti-socialist speeches: unless we believe that they are deliberate liars and imposters, who to serve their own interests labour to mislead other people, we must conclude that they do not understand Socialism. There is no other possible explanation of the extraordinary things they write and say. The thing they cry out against is not Socialism but a phantom of their own imagining.'

In Chapter 23, for example, Frankie explains that the Butcher

> '... didn't understand anything about Socialism himself - only that it meant sharing out all the money so that everyone could have the same.'

A similar argument is put forward by 'the man on the pail' in Chapter 25:

> '... as I said before, if all the money in the country was shared out equal today according to Owen's ideas - in six months' time it would be all back again in the same 'ands as it is now ...'

Further on, Owen responds to a similar argument presented by Crass in the form of a cutting from the Obscurer, entitled 'Prove Your Principles: Or, Look at Both Sides'

> 'It means that if the Editor of the Obscurer put that in his paper as an argument against Socialism, either he is of feeble intellect himself or else he thinks that the majority of his readers are.

Anti-socialist sentiments are also presented in the form of slurs during some of the speeches made in Chapter 44, to which Barrington offers the following rebuke:

> '... it would have been more to the point if Mr Grinder had taken some particular Socialist doctrine and had proved it to be untrue or misleading, instead of adopting the cowardly method of making vague general charges that he cannot substantiate.'

Undeterred, however, the workmen are still content to repeat similar charges in the next chapter:

> 'Socialism means, "What's yours is mine, and what's mine's me own,"' observed Bundy, and ... Slyme was heard to say that Socialism meant Materialism, Atheism and Free Love, and if it were ever to come about it would degrade men and women to the level of brute beasts ... Sawkins said that Socialism was a lot of bloody rot, and Crass expressed the opinion - which he had culled from the delectable columns of the Obscurer - that it meant robbing the industrious for the benefit of the idle and thriftless.'

Another unsubstantiated argument encountered by Owen is also recounted by the narrator in Chapter 40:

> 'All this talk about Socialism and State employment was frightening Capital out of the country. Those who had money were afraid to invest it in industries, or to

have any work done for fear they would be robbed.'

Nevertheless, not all opposition is idle talk. In a ruse, revealed in Chapter 30, the owners of the Electric Light Works decide to sell the failing concern to the local council, which they also happen to control. Their plan is not simply to recover their investments, however, it also has the added benefit of discrediting the idea of socialism:

> 'we're not only doin' ourselves a bit of good, but we're likewise doin' the Socialists a lot of 'arm. When the ratepayers 'ave bought the Works, and they begins to kick up a row because they're losin' money over it - we can tell 'em that it's Socialism! And then they'll say that if that's Socialism they don't want no more of it.'

21st Century

According to a *Prospect Magazine* article published on the eve of the 2019 General Election:

> 'A search through media database LexisNexis shows that since the election was called on October 29, some variation of the words "communist," "Marxist," "socialist," "Lenin,"' and "Stalin" have been used almost 2,400 times by the UK's biggest newspapers (The Daily Mail, The

Telegraph, The Times, The Financial Times, The Sun and The Guardian).'

In an editorial published on 21st November 2019, the Financial Times also opined:

> 'The Labour party manifesto is nothing more than a blueprint for socialism in one country. The combination of punitive tax increases, sweeping nationalisation, and the end of Thatcher-era union reforms turns the clock back 40 years. Set alongside a vast expansion of the state — based on spending amounting to six per cent of national income — Labour's plans are a recipe for terminal economic decline.'

The term 'broadband communism' was also used widely to characterize a Labour Party pledge to deliver free full-fibre broad band by 2030. Matthew Fell, Chief UK Policy Director at the Confederation of British Industry went even further, warning:

> 'As the scope of Labour's radical re-nationalisation plans expands almost daily, firms around the world lose confidence in the UK as a place to invest safely. Some will be asking if they are next. This threat damages the livelihoods of communities across the country. It's time for all parties to work with business, not against it.'

On the other hand, nationalization of unprofitable industries and corporations has a long history. Examples include:

Coal Mining, 1947
Rolls-Royce, 1971
British Leyland, 1975
Johnson Matthey Bank, 1984
Railtrack, 2002
HBOS, RBS and Lloyds TSB, 2008
East Coast Rail, 2018
Northern Rail, 2020

It is also worth noting that many 'privatized' entities are operated by state owned companies, such as: Arriva - a subsidiary of Germany's state-owned Deutsche Bahn, and Électricité de France otherwise known as EDF.

Apprentices

Tressell

There are three examples of apprenticeship in the novel, one with Rushton & Co. and two in Sweater's drapery business. The first involves Bert White, who in Chapter Seven we learn, was to be trained as a painter and decorator:

> 'At first Mr Rushton demanded ten pounds as a premium, the boy to be bound for five years, no wages the first year, two shillings a week the second, and a rise of one shilling every year for the remainder of the term. Afterwards, as a special favour - a matter of charity, in fact, as she was a very poor woman - he agreed to accept five pounds.'

Both of Sweater's endeavours are reported in Chapter 20, the first of which involved the employment of:

> '... a great number of girls and young women who were supposed to be learning dressmaking, mantle-making or millinery. These were all indentured apprentices, some of whom had paid premiums of from five to ten pounds. They were 'bound' for three years. For the first two years they received no wages ...'

We are also told that:

> 'This method of obtaining labour by false pretences and without payment, ... was adopted in other departments of his business. He procured shop assistants of both sexes on the same terms. A youth was indentured, usually for five years, to be "Made a Man of" and "Turned out fit to take a Position in any House". If possible, a premium, five, ten, or twenty pounds - according to their circumstances - would be extracted from the parents. For the first three years, no wages: after that, perhaps two or three shillings a week.'

All this provides a stark contrast with the original purpose of apprenticeship described by Barrington in Chapter 45:

> 'The apprentices were there to master the trade, qualifying themselves to become master workers themselves; not mere sweaters and exploiters of the labour of others, but useful members of society.'

21st Century

Apprentices and their families no longer have to pay a premium to employers, although an employer's training costs are subsidized by the tax-payer via an apprenticeship service account, or government employer co-investment. The apprentice is also guaranteed the minimum wage which, for apprentices aged 19 or under, was set at £3.90 an hour in April 2019.

Not every trainee is guaranteed to receive the minimum wage, however:

~ Anyone aged between 16 and 24 years old and undertaking a traineeship only receives expenses for travel and meals.
~ Jobseeker's Allowance or Universal Credit claimants doing work experience for 25 to 30 hours a week, only receive their normal benefit payments plus costs for travel or childcare.
~ The Department for Work and Pensions also arranges unpaid volunteering and work trials.
~ Internships that are less than a year and part of a higher education course are also exempt from the minimum wage

Unpaid internships are also available to those who can afford it. In January 2018, for example, The Sutton Trust Research Brief *Internships - Unpaid, Unadvertised, Unfair*, estimated that the minimum cost of a six-month internship in London was £6,603 and £5,313 in Manchester.

Causes of Poverty

Tressell

In the opening chapter of the book, Owen counters the causes put forward by his colleagues at the Cave:

> 'The theories that drunkenness, laziness or inefficiency are the causes of poverty are so many devices invented and fostered by those who are selfishly interested in maintaining the present states of affairs, for the purpose of preventing us from discovering the real causes of our present condition.'

Later, in Chapter 15, he returns to the explanations offered by his fellow workers:

> 'Poverty is not caused by men and women getting married; it's not caused by machinery; it's not caused by "over-production"; it's not caused by drink or laziness; and it's not caused by "over-population".'

His question from Chapter One: '... what is the cause of the lifelong poverty of the majority of those who are not drunkards and who DO work?' remains unanswered until Chapter 15, where he replies to Easton: 'The present system – competition – capitalism.'

Challenged to explain, he admits that: 'There are many causes, but they are all part of and inseparable from the system ...' before proceeding to identify:

> '... private ownership of land, private ownership of railways, tramways, gasworks, waterworks, private ownership of factories, and the other means of producing the necessaries and comforts of life. Competition in business -'

Later in the chapter, this is explained:

> 'The successful tenderer has usually cut the price so fine that to make it pay he has to scamp the work, pay low wages, and drive and sweat the men whom he employs.'

And developed:

> '... this competition of the employers is one of the causes of unemployment and poverty, because it's not only in our line - exactly the same thing happens in every other trade and industry. Competing employers are the upper and nether millstones which grind the workers between them.'

Similarly, Chapter One makes reference to how workers compete for employment:

> 'Why, if all the drunkards and won't-works and unskilled or inefficient workers could

be by some miracle transformed into sober, industrious and skilled workers tomorrow, it would, under the present conditions, be so much the worse for us, because there isn't enough work for all NOW and those people by increasing the competition for what work there is, would inevitably cause a reduction of wages and a greater scarcity of employment.'

21st Century

Although not stated explicitly, income-based methods used to define and measure POVERTY, such as the Department for Work and Pensions' 'Households Below Average Income' yardstick, hint at its principal cause. Paradoxically, however, they are also used to associate the causes of poverty with socio-economic circumstances, events and the choices made by those affected. In other words, the symptoms of the disease are mistakenly identified as its causes.

The Child Poverty Action Group, for example, identify: costs of housing and childcare, low pay, lack of work, and inadequate social security. The terms 'lack of work' and 'worklessness' are applied to temporary and part-time employment and to people who are prevented from working due to ill-health and/ or caring responsibilities. To all intents and purposes, though, the idea that poverty is the result of not working enough, plays into the narratives that poor people are lazy, and that the solution is - as Tressell's philanthropists might say – 'plenty of work.'

Since the financial crash of 2008, wage stagnation is also cited as a contributory factor. Low wage growth is also considered to be a consequence of technological change and automation that increases competition between workers who have fewer qualifications and skills; a situation compounded by the lack of opportunities for promotion or increased earnings. Perhaps a more pertinent observation would be that, in spite of a statutory minimum wage, work is and never has been a route out of poverty, as evidenced by the numbers of working families who rely on state benefits and foodbanks.

In much the same way as Labour's *New Deal for Lone Parents* bought into the idea that young single parents were a cause of poverty, the Conservative and Liberal Democrat Government effectively rebranded the approach with its 2012 *Troubled Families Programme*. This new initiative adopted a pro-active approach whereby support workers were required to intervene in the affairs of families deemed to be in need of assistance. This included 'Employment Support' a scheme designed to move people into work (having 'an adult on out-of-work benefits' being a definition of a troubled family) and advice for families struggling to manage their MONEY and DEBT.

Meanwhile, according to groups like Disability Rights UK, the Joseph Rowntree Foundation, Shelter etc. Government policy choices, such as reductions in funding for public services and cuts to benefits and tax credits - so-called austerity - are also considered to have removed the 'safety net' designed to prevent people from falling into poverty. Similar conclusions were also drawn by Professor Philip Alston, United Nations Special Rapporteur on extreme poverty and human rights in his *Statement on Visit to the United Kingdom.*

Charity

Tressell

Although the examples of charitable relief are by and large fictitious, reference is made in Chapter One to the work of the Salvation Army:

> 'Hundreds are found work daily. Soup and bread are distributed in the midnight hours to homeless wanderers in London. Additional workshops for the unemployed have been established.'

In Chapter 36, Mugsborough's Organized Benevolence Society is introduced as the recipient of:

> '... about three hundred pounds in hard cash. This money was devoted to the relief of cases of distress.
>
> The largest item in the expenditure of the Society was the salary of the General Secretary, Mr Sawney Grinder – a most deserving case - who was paid one hundred pounds a year.'

Further on, Tressell's disdain is made plain:

> 'Meantime, in spite of this and kindred organizations the conditions of the underpaid poverty stricken and unemployed workers remained the same. ... the existence of the societies prevented the problem being grappled with in a sane and

> practical manner. The people lacked the necessaries of life: the necessaries of life are produced by Work: these people were willing to work, but were prevented from doing so by the idiotic system of society which these "charitable" people are determined to do their best to perpetuate.'

And hammered home:

> 'If the people who expect to be praised and glorified for being charitable were never to give another farthing it would be far better for the industrious poor, because then the community as a whole would be compelled to deal with the absurd and unnecessary state of affairs that exists today - millions of people living and dying in wretchedness and poverty in an age when science and machinery have made it possible to produce such an abundance of everything that everyone might enjoy plenty and comfort.'

This observation is also reinforced by Barrington in Chapter 45:

> 'The hundreds of thousands of pounds that are yearly wasted in well-meant but useless charity accomplish no lasting good, because while charity soothes the symptoms it ignores the disease, which is - the PRIVATE OWNERSHIP of the means

of producing the necessaries of life, and the restriction of production, by a few selfish individuals for their own profit.'

All of which makes a mockery of the assertion attributed to the 'charity-mongers' in Chapter 37, who claimed that: '... they were willing to give more in voluntary charity ...' than they were in taxes.

21st Century

According to the Charity Commission there were 183,681 charities in England and Wales as of 30th September 2018. Their total income for that year was £74.3 **billion.** The Office of the Scottish Charities Regulator has 24,824 charities registered, with a total annual income of £14 **billion**.

The *Pay and Equalities Survey 2019*, conducted by the Association of Chief Executives of Voluntary Organisations, also estimated the average salary for Charity Chief Executives was £52,000 in 2018.

More specifically, those charities that operate with a similar purpose to the Organized Benevolence Society can be searched on the Charity Commission and Scottish Regulator websites and are as follows:

In England and Wales there are 33,150 charities whose purpose is the prevention or relief of POVERTY. For Scotland the figure is 3,725.

South of the border, there are also 172 bodies engaged in work with homeless people and 166 in Scotland. (See HOMELESSNESS.)

According to the House of Commons Briefing Paper 8585, there were over 2,000 foodbanks operating in the UK in 2019. Responsible for these operations were 267 organisations registered in England and Wales, plus 47 in Scotland.

During 2018-19, the Trussell Trust alone distributed 1,583,668 food parcels across the UK. In Scotland, the Independent Food Aid Network and A Menu for Change recorded 84 independent foodbanks issuing 221,977 food parcels between April 2017 and September 2018. Over the same period, 118 Trussell Trust foodbanks also allocated 258,606.

Debt

Tressell

The type of debt described in the novel, is often an informal arrangement with local traders, that is designed to facilitate the characters subsistence. In Chapter Two, for example, the desperate circumstances of an anonymous unemployed man are recounted:

> 'Last winter they had got into debt; that was nothing unusual, but owing to the bad summer they had not been able, as in other years, to pay off the debts accumulated in winter. It was doubtful, too, whether they would be able to get credit again this winter. In fact this morning when his wife sent their little girl to the grocer's for some butter the latter had refused to let the child have it without the money.'

Later in the book, we are told how the main protagonist suffers a similar fate:

> '... Owen earned nothing, and to make matters worse the grocer from whom they usually bought their things suddenly refused to let them have any more credit. Owen went to see him, and the man said he was very sorry, but he could not let them have anything more without the money; he did not mind waiting a few

> weeks for what was already owing, but he could not let the amount get any higher; his books were full of bad debts already. ... he repeated several times that his books were full of bad debts and his own creditors were pressing him.' (Chapter 34)

During an argument over MONEY in Chapter Three, Ruth Easton refutes her husband's accusations of poor housekeeping:

> 'When you're not working, we must either get into debt or starve.'

Of course, debts accrued on food were compounded by arrears owed to landlords, such as in the case of the Newmans in Chapter 16:

> 'They still owed several weeks' rent, and were already so much in debt to the baker and the grocer that it was hopeless to expect any further credit.'

And the Owens in Chapter 51:

> 'Every week most of the money went to pay arrears of rent or some other debts, so that even whilst he was at work they had often to go without some of the necessaries of life.'

William Easton is again the foil in Chapter 13, this time for Owen to explain:

'... when there's no work, you will either starve or get into debt. When - as at present - there is a little work, you will live in a state of semi-starvation. When times are what you call "good", you will work for twelve or fourteen hours a day and - if you're VERY lucky - occasionally all night. The extra money you then earn will go to pay your debts so that you may be able to get credit again when there's no work.'

21st Century

The Office of National Statistics survey of *Household debt in Great Britain April 2016 to March 2018* found that a colossal total of £1.28 *trillion* was owed.

This included £119 *billion* (9%) which was made up of: overdrafts; loans; credit and store cards; mail order, hire purchase; student loans; arrears on credit commitments; and unpaid household bills.

The remainder, £1.16 *trillion* (91%), was loans that had been secured against a main residence or other privately-owned property, such as mortgages and equity release.

The study also found that unsecured, financial debt was more likely to be held by the least wealthy households and that it represented a comparatively large proportion of their total wealth. Meanwhile, two-thirds of people who struggled to keep up with debt repayments or other household bills, were most likely to be renting their home.

A more recent phenomenon of short-term or 'payday' lending at extortionate rates of interest is also a major source of debt. According to the Financial Conduct Authority report: *Consumer credit — high-cost short-term credit lending data*, there were more than 5.4 million loans of this kind in the 12 months prior to 30 June 2018 and these accounted for £1.2 **billion** of borrowing.

Fatalism

Tressell

There is a central paradox that revolves around the conditions in which the 'philanthropists' exist and their acceptance of their plight. People are described as being: 'clothed in rags,' on the verge of destitution, or in want and yet seemingly content with the fact that:

> 'they and their children had been all their lives on the verge of starvation and nakedness ...' (Chapter 25)

Earlier in the piece, in Chapter Four, the dilemma confronting Owen is elaborated in the following way:

> 'Thousands of people like himself dragged out a wretched existence on the very verge of starvation, and for the greater number of people life was one long struggle against POVERTY. Yet practically none of these people knew or even troubled themselves to inquire why they were in that condition; and for anyone else to try to explain to them was a ridiculous waste of time, for they did not want to know.'

The most frequent response from the men is bemoaned by Harlow in Chapter 25 and repeated word for word by 'the man behind the moat' in Chapter 45:

> 'There's always been rich and poor in the world and there always will be.'

In this, Harlow is supported by Slyme who inadvertently reveals the origin of the motto:

> 'It says in the Bible that the poor shall always be with us.'

The 'man behind the moat' also adds:

> 'You can't change 'uman nature, you know,'

Sarcastically, the narrative voice chides these submissive sentiments:

> 'At this, everybody brightened up again, and exchanged looks of satisfaction and relief. Of course! It wasn't necessary to think about these things at all! Nothing could ever be altered: it had always been more or less the same, and it always would be.

Perhaps some of the older men, had been worn down by their life of drudgery and struggling to survive. Like 'old Linden' in Chapter One, for example:

> 'It can't never be haltered,' interrupted old Linden. 'I don't see no sense in all this 'ere talk. There's always been rich and poor in the world, and there always will be.'

No such excuse is open to Easton, a younger man, who in Chapter 15 sees resistance as futile:

> 'We can't 'elp ourselves. If one man won't do it there's twenty others ready to take 'is place.'

He is therefore rebuked by Owen:

> 'We could help ourselves to a certain extent if we would stand by each other. If, for instance, we all belonged to the Society,'

Later in Chapter 43, however, the attitude toward unionization is described as follows:

> 'Ninety-nine out of every hundred of them did not believe in such things as those: they had much more sense than to join Trades Unions: on the contrary, they believed in placing themselves entirely at the mercy of their good, kind Liberal and Tory masters.

Sarcasm is used repeatedly to ridicule the fatalism of the workers:

> 'Therefore Crass and his mates, although they knew nothing whatever about it themselves, accepted it as an established, incontrovertible fact that the existing state of things is immutable. They believed it because someone else told them so. They would have believed anything: on one condition - namely, that they were told to believe it by their betters. They said it was surely not for the Like of Them to think

that they knew better than those who were more educated and had plenty of time to study.' (Chapter 21)

'And then, strangest fact of all, the people who find it a hard struggle to live, or who exist in dreadful poverty and sometimes starve, instead of trying to understand the causes of their misery and to find out a remedy themselves, spend all their time applauding the Practical, Sensible, Level-headed Business-men, who bungle and mismanage their affairs, and pay them huge salaries for doing so.' (Chapter 37)

Toward the end of the book, in Chapter 45, Barrington challenges the idea that things have always been like they are and cannot be changed:

'... it is not true that even in its essential features, the present system has existed from all time...'

'... the change from Feudalism into the earlier form of Capitalism; and the equally great change from what might be called the individualistic capitalism which displaced Feudalism, to the system of Co-operative Capitalism and Wage Slavery of today.'

> 'So it is not true that practically the same state of affairs as we have today has always existed.'

The view expressed in Chapter 48 is somewhat pessimistic however:

> 'The only things they feel any real interest in are beer, football, betting and - of course - one other subject. Their highest ambition is to be allowed to Work. And they desire nothing better for their children!'

21st Century

The repetitive use of slogans like 'the poor are always with us,' 'you can't change human nature' or 'it's common sense' is both a reinforcement and reflection of the reality that individuals who are excluded from decision-making have little or no power to change their immediate conditions. This point is explored by Noam Chomsky and developed in reference to spectator sport in *Understanding Power*.

The citation of documents as sources of authority, such the Christian new testament, is also a way of avoiding challenge. Matthew, 26:11 and Mark, 14:7, for example, use the phrase 'For you always have the poor with you,' but its meaning is open to interpretation. For those of a conservative or passive bent, it will be taken to mean that the existence of poverty is a natural state of things that cannot or should not be altered. According to an alternative reading, however, it is an affirmation that the disciples of Jesus will be supported by the poor.

Alongside a fostered sense of inevitability, helplessness and resignation for some lies the social dynamic of distraction. The drive to achieve, accomplish, consume, perform and possess is constantly reinforced. Contact with the world is mediated through mobile devices and apps, while entertainment and news are fused into stories about celebrity, scandal and other trivia. Decision making and evaluation is deferred to 'experts' who are seemingly ignorant of historical context beyond what is new.

In the meantime, trade union membership peaked at 13.2 million in 1979, but has fallen since. According to the *Trade Union Membership: Statistical Bulletin* 6.35 million or 23.4% of working people belonged to a union in 2018 – a figure almost identical to a membership of six and a half million in 1918. Today, 3.69 million union members work in the public sector, compared to 2.66 in the private sector and 3.5 million women members. It is also the case that the larger the workplace, the more likely workers will join a union.

Foreigners

Tressell

When the characters are discussing the CAUSES OF POVERTY in Chapter One, we are told that Easton:

> '... was conscious of a growing feeling of indignation and hatred against foreigners of every description, who were ruining this country...'

Crass also offers a similar opinion:

> '... you know very well that the country IS being ruined by foreigners.'

Sawkins chimes in support:

> 'We're overrun with 'em! Nearly all the waiters and the cook at the Grand Hotel where we was working last month is foreigners.'

Joe Philpot, provides some colourful anecdotes:

> '... and then thers all them Hitalian horgin grinders, an' the blokes wot sells 'ot chestnuts; an' wen I was goin' 'ome last night I see a lot of them Frenchies sellin' hunions, an' a little wile afterwards I met two more of 'em comin' up the street with a bear.'

Harlow introduces a well-worn euphemism:

> 'The greatest cause of poverty is hover-population...'

Lastly, by way of explanation, the narrative voice provides context:

> 'The papers they read were filled with vague and alarming accounts of the quantities of foreign merchandise imported into this country, the enormous number of aliens constantly arriving, and their destitute conditions, how they lived, the crimes they committed, and the injury they did to British trade. These were the seeds which, cunningly sown in their minds, caused to grow up within them a bitter undiscriminating hatred of foreigners. ... The country was in a hell of a state, poverty, hunger and misery in a hundred forms had already invaded thousands of homes and stood upon the thresholds of thousands more. How came these things to be? It was the bloody foreigner! Therefore, down with the foreigners and all their works. Out with them. Drive them b**s into the bloody sea!
>
> ... The foreigner was the enemy, and the cause of poverty and bad trade.'

21st Century

The idea that all the problems faced by Britain are the fault of asylum seekers, migrants, refugees, the European Union and health tourists has a number of exponents. It is epitomized by the 2013 conference speech of then leader of the United Kingdom Independence Party (UKIP) who claimed that Britain was absorbing 5 million economic migrants over a ten-year period. This, he claimed, was responsible for problems faced by public services, including schools and the NHS. Migrants were also said to be the cause of house price inflation and the undercutting of wages.

In line with this agenda, the Conservative and Liberal Democrat Government introduced a minimum income rule which had to be met before British citizens could bring non-European spouses into the country. They also required landlords, doctors, Banks, the DVLA and employers to check immigration status and instigated Operation Vaken. Under this scheme, immigration enforcement vehicles were given the appearance of police cars, adverts were placed in newspapers, shops and buildings used by certain faith groups, and vans were sent around the streets of London with the warning: 'Go home or face arrest.' The impact of this approach is recorded in Liberty's 2019 publication: *A Guide to the Hostile Environment*.

The climate of hostility toward 'foreigners' is fully reflected in the printed MEDIA. Analysis conducted by *The New European*, for example, found that in 2016 there were 277 front page stories with an anti-immigration slant and over half of these involved the *Daily Mail* and *Daily Express*. Further investigation showed that those two papers alone carried 1,768 pages of stories related to immigration, race relations and treatment of foreigners, with many of the themes reflecting the sentiments advocated by UKIP and put into practice by the Conservatives and Liberal Democrats.

Free Trade

Tressell

The recurring themes of 'free trade' and 'tariff reform' i.e. protection, are indicative of the political allegiance of the story's characters. Conservative supporters' favour the latter and Liberals advocate the former. This is presented as a choice between 'Tariff Reform and Plenty of Work' and 'Free Trade and Cheap Food,' as offered by the parliamentary candidates in Chapter 48.

There are some doubters, however, such as Philpot who chairs the 'Great Oration' in Chapter 45:

> 'Now, some people tells us as the way to put everything right is to 'ave Free Trade and plenty of cheap food. Well, we've got them all now, but the misery seems to go on all around us all the same. Then there's other people tells us as the 'Friscal Policy' is the thing to put everything right.'

Owen is an opponent of both and, in the opening chapter, he characterizes the choice as follows:

> 'We've had Free Trade for the last fifty years and today most people are living in a condition of more or less abject poverty, and thousands are literally starving. When we had Protection things were worse still. Other countries have

Protection and yet many of their people are glad to come here and work for starvation wages. The only difference between Free Trade and Protection is that under certain circumstances one might be a little worse than the other ...'

21st Century

Free Trade is once again being offered as a panacea for Britain's ills. According to the Economists for Free Trade report *In One Bound We Can Be Free*, for example, the benefits include: lower UK prices, raised productivity through competition, higher wages and increased employment. In this scenario, a free trade deal with the United States is projected to increase UK GDP by 4%, raises economic output by £80 billion and reduce consumer prices by 8%. This model is premised on removing what the group call 'trade barriers,' such as: administration systems, duties, import controls, licensing, public procurement, quotas, regulations (presumably consumer, animal welfare and environmental protections), subsidies and tariffs.

This approach appears to be utopian in its assumption that countries like Japan and the USA will end subsidies to domestic agricultural, clothing and textile production, even though the World Trade Organization has spent over 25 years attempting to negotiate a workable *Agreement on Agriculture*. Similarly, no mention is made of the trade that takes place within multinational corporations and between their subsidiaries at managed rather than market mechanisms and prices, or whether it will still be possible for corporations to sue nation states for compensation.

Freedom

Tressell

The ideal of individual or personal liberty as promoted in the American and French constitutions is referred to with disdain by the narrator. The conditions experienced by Mr Sweater's homeworkers in Chapter 20, for example, are deemed to be fair, because:

> 'No one is compelled to accept any particular set of conditions in a free country like this.'

In Chapter 25, we are told sardonically that workers are better off than slaves, because:

> '... he enjoys the priceless blessing of Freedom. If he does not like the hirer's conditions he need not accept them. He can refuse to work, and he can go and starve. There are no ropes on him. He is a Free man. He is the Heir of all the Ages. He enjoys perfect Liberty. He has the right to choose freely which he will do - Submit or Starve. Eat dirt or eat nothing.'

In contrast, we learn in Chapter 40 that: 'No one felt free from observation for a single moment' Then, three chapters later: '... each one was given a time-sheet on which he was required to account for every minute of the day' and therefore 'A reign of terror - the terror of the sack – prevailed.'

Ultimately, therefore they:

> '... were not free: their servile lives were spent in grovelling and cringing and toiling and running about like little dogs at the behest of their numerous masters.'
> (Chapter 44)

21st Century

Wage-labourers are still theoretically able to refuse to work and starve – as in the case of people who have been sanctioned by the Department for Work and Pensions, but in the workplace an employee has little or no control over their activities and no right to the product of their creativity. Performance is also monitored, albeit the methods of surveillance are now more unobtrusive and comprehensive. Computerised offices and factories, for example, use software to monitor workflow processes and worker behaviour.

Outside the workplace, *Which?* magazine reports that devices called 'smart,' 'personalised,' or 'assistant' that are connected to the internet are likely to be collecting and transmitting data about the people using them. The information collected is used for targeted advertising, but also to shape behaviour toward particular commercial products and therefore profitability. Of course, this undermines the free market ideal of traders having a perfect knowledge of price, quality and competition, but it also negates notions that the will of an individual can be expressed in the marketplace, or that a consumer has the right to choose what to buy.

The nature, development and implications of such practices are explored by Shoshana Zuboff's *The Age of Surveillance Capitalism*, including the cross-over into state surveillance. In Britain, in May 2018, for example, South Wales police used Automated Facial Recognition to scan crowds at BBC Radio 1's Biggest Weekend in Swansea and at the 2017 Champions League final in Cardiff. 'Facial analysis' technology is also used to examine facial expressions, posture, gestures and movement to identify 'suspicious' behaviour. Such techniques can also be used by retailers to analyse personal reactions to products and add this data to the predictive data already gathered via 'bonus,' 'club' and other 'loyalty' schemes.

Hire System

Tressell

Otherwise known as Hire Purchase, HP, Instalment Plan and, more colloquially, 'the never-never,' the hire system is a form of credit and therefore DEBT. Usually used by people who can't afford to buy an item outright, they make a down-payment and pay off the balance – including interest – over an agreed period. In this way, they have use of an article, but the seller retains ownership until the balance is paid in full.

In Chapter 25, for example, Owen remarks caustically:

> 'If you see a workman wearing a really good suit of clothes you may safely conclude that he ... has obtained it from a tallyman on the hire system and has not yet paid for it.'

The Easton's financial struggles are laid bare in Chapter Three, where we learn that:

> 'The table, oilcloth, fender, hearthrug, etc, had been obtained on the hire system and were not yet paid for.'

Having fallen behind on their payments, they receive a reminder from Didlum & Co. prompting the following exasperated comment:

> 'Now we'll have this bloody debt dragging on us for years, and before the dam stuff is paid for it'll be worn out.'

This company is described in Chapter 40, as having '… a large hire system trade,' from which they profit twice over:

> 'He had an extensive stock of second-hand furniture that he had resumed possession of when the unfortunate would-be purchasers failed to pay the instalments regularly.'

21st Century

The Office of National Statistics survey of *Household debt in Great Britain April 2016 to March 2018* records total Hire Purchase debt as £25 **billion.** In other words, 4.6 million households were recorded as holding some form of hire purchase debt with a median figure of £3,500.

Other forms of 'hire system' are also evident in modern day Britain. In the *2019 Annual Review* published by the British Vehicle Rental and Leasing Association, for example, the vehicle rental and leasing industry is said to have an annual worth of £49 **billion**.

Telecommunications represents another area of regular consumer spending, with Ofcom estimating that households spent an average of £83.56 per month in 2018. A significant element of which were the 20 million monthly mobile phone contracts that included an estimated charge of £18.52 per month for a handset.

Homelessness

Tressell

Among the many examples of POVERTY and destitution recounted in the novel, the lack of a place to sleep is mentioned only twice. It is first referred to in Chapter 29, when Bert White describes a 'very beautiful scene':

> '..."Early Morning in Trafalgar Square". Ere we see a lot of Englishmen who have been sleepin' out all night because they ain't got no 'omes to go to.'

The second reference is in Chapter 40, where the narrative voice records the following paradox:

> 'One of the things that the human race needed in order to exist was shelter; so with much painful labour they had constructed a large number of houses. Thousands of these houses were now standing unoccupied, while millions of the people who had helped to build the houses were either homeless or herding together in overcrowded hovels.'

21st Century

According to the housing charity *Shelter* for every 200 people living in Britain, there is at least one homeless person. Its report *This is England: A picture of homelessness in 2019* estimates that on any given night in 2019 over 280,000 people were homeless in England alone. In the UK as a whole the suggested figure is at least 320,000, which includes:

~ People sleeping rough.
~ Single people living in hostels, shelters, women's refuges and temporary supported accommodation.
~ Statutorily homeless households – those who are recognized as being in 'priority need' and are therefore owed a duty by their local authority.

It does not, however, cover people classed as 'Hidden homeless,' such as those who make informal arrangements with family and friends to sleep on sofas or floors, as well as people living in squats, cars, sheds, or Bed & Breakfast accommodation.

Furthermore, the Office for National Statistics report *Deaths of homeless people in England and Wales: 2018*, estimates that 726 homeless people died in that year.

Landlordism

Tressell

On several occasions Tressell emphasizes the burden of household rent. In chapter 28, for example, we are told the amounts that people paid: 'The Newmans lived in a small house the rent of which was six shillings per week and taxes.' While, later in the same chapter we learn that the Owens' weekly rent was seven shillings.

In the following chapter, during his Pandorama show, Bert White tells the children: '... most of the money wot the bloke earns 'as to pay the rent.' A message that is repeated in Chapter 33 in reference to Jack Linden's daughter-in-law: 'Most of the money she earned went to pay the rent' and again in Chapter 54 where we are told that for Owen: 'Most of the money he earned went for rent' and that: 'about a third of the wages of the working classes were paid away as rent and rates.'

Identifying 'Landlordism' as one of the CAUSES OF POVERTY, in Chapter 15, Owen explains:

> '... Under the present system the country belongs to a few ... they allow the majority to remain in the land on one condition - that is, they must pay rent to the few for the privilege of being permitted to live in the land of their birth. The amount of rent demanded by those who own this country

is so large that, in order to pay it, the greater number of the majority have often to deprive themselves and their children, not only of the comforts, but even the necessaries of life. In the case of the working classes the rent absorbs at the lowest possible estimate, about one-third of their total earnings, for it must be remembered that the rent is an expense that goes on all the time, whether they are employed or not. If they get into arrears when out of work, they have to pay double when they get employment again.'

Another form of rental obligation is identified in Chapter 25:

'... exorbitant prices are charged for the articles they sell, to enable the proprietors to amass fortunes, and to pay extortionate rents to the landlords. That is why the wages and salaries of nearly all those who do the work created by these businesses are cut down to the lowest possible point.'

In the same chapter, Crass tells us: 'the earth belongs to the landlords!' and in Chapter Five the position and attitude of Jack Linden is recounted:

'During the thirty years of his tenancy he had paid altogether nearly six hundred pounds in rent, more than double the amount of the present value of the house.

Jack did not complain of this ... He often said that Mr Sweater was a very good landlord, because on several occasions when, being out of work, he had been a few weeks behind with his rent the agent acting for the benevolent Mr Sweater had allowed Linden to pay off the arrears by instalments. As old Jack was in the habit of remarking, many a landlord would have sold up their furniture and turned them into the street.'

21ˢᵗ Century

By and Large, Britain is still privately owned, but the composition is now slightly different. To the traditional aristocratic heredity, we can now add parvenu industrialists and financiers, as well as foreign owned corporations and those registered in tax-havens. An on-line 2018 article *The Uk's 50 Biggest Landowners Revealed*, for example, lists seven privatized water utilities that own huge swathes of land totalling over 400,000 acres. The ownership of these corporations is also global, stretching as far afield as Abu Dhabi, Australia, Canada, China, Hong Kong and Kuwait.

While ownership details are important, the crucial factor is still the exercise of influence and power over communities, families and individuals that such concentrations of wealth permit. According to a 2019 report by the Affordable Housing Commission -

Defining and measuring housing affordability – an alternative approach – there are 2.9 million households struggling pay their rent, compared to 900,000 homeowners who face housing cost issues.

The same report also shows that 270,000 private sector tenants, who are in the lower half of earners, face rent costs that account for 33 to 39% of their income, compared to 170,000 who live in social housing. These figures even increase to 950,000 and 210,000 respectively, for people whose rent charge represents 40% or more of their income.

Those struggling to afford their rent are also unlikely to be able to afford accommodation with seperate rooms for each of their children. They also have to pay rent, even when the accommodation is considered to be sub-standard; as is the case for 270,000 private sector tenants and 40,000 in social housing who pay more than a third of their income in rent.

Living Wage

Tressell

The term is used by Tressell to signify a level of subsistence, as in Chapter 23:

> 'After he has been working ten or twenty years he commands no more than he did at first - a bare living wage - sufficient money to purchase fuel to keep the human machine working.'

A point repeated by Barrington in Chapter 44:

> 'All through those twenty years they have earned but a bare living wage and have had to endure such privations that those who are not already dead are broken in health.'

In the following chapter, the writers for Tory and Liberal papers are said to believe that the basis of a civilized nation is:

> 'For the majority of the people to work like brutes in order to obtain a 'living wage' for themselves ...'

This idea of a living wage is summed up in Chapter 23:

> '... all they have to do is to give him enough money to provide him with food and clothing - of a kind - while he is working for them. If they only make him ill, they will not have to feed him or provide him

with medical care while he is laid up. He will either go without these things or pay for them himself.'

The wages system is therefore considered to be a way in which workers conned by their employers:

'... the working class, who spend all their wages in buying back only a very small part of the things they produce. Therefore what remains in the possession of their masters represents the difference between the value of the work done and the wages paid for doing it.' (Chapter 25)

The point is developed in the same Chapter by Owen:

'... as the money is of no use, the workers go to shops and give it away in exchange for some of the things they themselves have made. They spend - or give back - ALL their wages; but as the money they got as wages is not equal in value to the things they produced, they find that they are only able to buy back a VERY SMALL PART.

'Their wages are supposed to be equal in value to their work. But it's not so. If it were, by spending all their wages, the producing class would be able to buy back All they had produced.

'If their wages were really equal in value to the product of their labour ... they would be able to buy back not a small part - but the Whole.

'The total value of the wealth produced in this country during the last year was £1,800,000,000, and the total amount paid in wages during the same period was only £600,000,000. In other words, by means of the Money Trick, the workers were robbed of two-thirds of the value of their labour.'

21ˢᵗ Century

Since April 2016, Britons have benefited from two levels of 'Living Wage.' In 2001, for example, the Living Wage Foundation began campaigning for an hourly rate which it calculates will provide people with a minimum acceptable living standard. The second rate is touted as a 'national living wage' by the UK Government, but it only applies to people over 25 years of age and is set at 60% of median earnings.

Fundamentally, therefore, the concept of a 'Living Wage' represents a level of subsistence or, in the words of the Living Wage campaign: 'what people need to get by.' The 2019 report: *Calculating a Living Wage for London and the rest of the UK*, explains how they arrive at the level of income needed, but it is pitched at employers who can 'afford' to pay it. In similar fashion, the *Low Pay Commission 2019 Report* considers 'whether the economy can bear a higher minimum wage' as well as considering 'the affordability of the National Living Wage to individual firms.'

What this means in practice, is that however a 'living wage' is calculated, it is not intended to equal the value of the wealth created by people at work. Similarly, it does nothing to challenge the mystifying function of MONEY.

Machinery

Tressell

The impact of mechanization on the number of jobs and the living standards of the workers is first raised in Chapter One by Crass:

> 'Then thers all this new-fangled machinery,' continued Crass. 'That's wot's ruinin' everything. Even in our trade ther's them machines for trimmin' wallpaper, an' now they've brought out a paintin' machine. Ther's a pump an' a 'ose pipe, an' they reckon two men can do as much with this 'ere machine as twenty could without it.'

The topic is discussed further in Chapter Seven, where Crass repeats the phrase: 'new-fangled machinery' before adding:

> 'You can't expect there can be plenty of work for everyone with all this 'ere labour-savin' machinery what's been invented.'

Supported in his argument by Harlow, Crass is then emboldened:

> 'That's just what I say. Machinery is the real cause of the poverty. That's what I said the other day.'

As the discussion unfolds, these views are challenged by Owen:

> 'Machinery is undoubtedly the cause of unemployment, ... but it's not the cause of poverty: that's another matter altogether.'

> 'If you think that the machinery, which makes it possible to produce all the necessaries of life in abundance, is the cause of the shortage, it seems to me that there must be something the matter with your minds.'

Quoting figures from 'the Daily Mail Year Book for 1907, page 33, Owen continues:

> '"It is a very noticeable fact that although the number of factories and their value have vastly increased in the United Kingdom, there is an absolute decrease in the number of men and women employed in those factories between 1895 and 1901. This is doubtless due to the displacement of hand labour by machinery!"

A little later, he develops his point:

> 'As we have seen, a great deal of the work which was formerly done by human beings is now being done by machinery. This machinery belongs to a few people: it is worked for the benefit of those few, just the same as were the human beings it displaced.'

This point is reiterated by Barrington in Chapter 45:

> '... the machinery became the property of a comparatively few individuals and private companies, who use it not for the benefit of the community but to create profits for themselves.'

21st Century

In the latter part of the Twentieth Century, factories and offices were transformed by computerization and the development of the microchip. Jack Jones makes reference to this in his 1984 lecture *Robert Tressell's Message for Today*, while Paul Mason in *Postcapitalism*, discusses other examples including how the construction and design of aircraft was affected. More recently, the social impact of these changes has extended beyond the workplace into everyday living, with the next phase - dubbed the Fourth Industrial Revolution - forecast to revolutionize the use of artificial intelligence, automation and robotics, in ways that will not only replace working people, but also negate their ability to earn and therefore consume.

According to the Office of National Statistics' analysis of working people in 2017, *Which occupations are at highest risk of being automated?* the jobs of 7.4% were considered to be at high risk of automation. At the other end of the spectrum, 27.7% of workers' jobs were thought to have a low risk, while the vast majority 64.9% were considered to be at medium risk. Meanwhile, *How robots change the world* a report by Oxford Economics predicts that the greatest impact will be felt in rural areas where manufacturing activity is concentrated in small towns.

In the retail sector, the full implications of "Just Walk Out" technology being trialled in Amazon Go shops in the United States is yet to be realised. It is touted as a checkout-free shopping experience, that uses surveillance cameras, weight sensors and deep learning technology to detect products taken from shelves and record them in a virtual basket. Entry to the shop is via the Amazon Go mobile app, and when a shopper leaves, their Amazon account is debited and a receipt sent to the app.

Media

Tressell

We are introduced to the organs of the local media through conversations between the characters, but it is not until Chapter 30, that we learn:

> The three local papers were run by limited companies. Sweater held nearly all the shares of the Ananias and of the Weekly Chloroform, and controlled their policy and contents. Grinder occupied the same position with regard to the Obscurer. The editors were a sort of marionettes who danced as Sweater and Grinder pulled the strings.'

This sheds light on comments made by Crass during a discussion on the CAUSES OF POVERTY, and related matters in Chapter One:

> 'I reads the Ananias every week, and I generally takes the Daily Chloroform, or the Hobscurer, so I ought to know summat about it.'

Later his faith in such publications is confirmed by the narrator in Chapter Seven: 'If it wasn't right, a paper like that would never have printed it.'

Even Owen drew some pleasure from the trivia that passed as news:

> 'Here was something to distract his thoughts: if not instructive or comforting, it would at any rate be interesting and even amusing to read the reports of the self-satisfied, futile talk of the profound statesmen who with comical gravity presided over the working of the Great System which their combined wisdom pronounced to be the best that could possibly be devised.' (Chapter Six)

These papers, however, are shown to be pursuing a set agenda, such as when the owners are planning to sell the Electric Light Supply company to the local Corporation in Chapter 30, and agree to:

> 'arrange to 'ave a lot of letters sent "To the Editor of the Obscurer" and "To the Editor of the Ananias," and "To the Editor of the Weekly Chloroform" in favour of the scheme.'

Likewise, we are told that Easton is reading some 'some carefully cooked statistics relating to Free Trade and Protection' from the Obscurer in Chapter One. Although:

> '... he was not about to understand exactly what the compiler of the figures was driving at - probably the latter never intended that anyone should understand ..'

In more general terms, Chapter 45 begins with the following:

> 'The Tory papers ... published yards of misleading articles about Tariff Reform. The Liberal papers said Tariff Reform was no remedy.'

And a little later:

> 'Most of the writers of these Liberal and Tory papers seemed to think that all that was necessary was to find 'Work' for the 'working' class! That was their conception of a civilized nation in the twentieth century!'

Such writers are referred to with disdain in Chapter 37 as 'hired scribes of the capitalist Press'

21st Century

A Media Reform Coalition 2019 report: *Who Owns the UK Media?* identify three companies that own 83% of national newspapers: News UK publishes the Times and Sun, DMG is publisher of the Daily Mail and Metro, and Reach plc owns the Mirror, People, Express and Star. In terms of online content, these three are joined by the Guardian and Telegraph to account for 80% of output. Similarly, local newspaper publishing is dominated by US based Gannett, JPI Media, Trinity Mirror, Tindle Newspapers, and Archant.

When it comes to telecommunications, there is no comparator, but private domination if not MONOPOLY is still evident. Commercial radio, local analogue and digital stations, for example, are dominated by Bauer, Global and Celador Radio. Sky UK (now owned by US firm Comcast), on the other hand, is the largest broadcaster and has the lion's share of pay to watch television, followed by BT, Apple, Amazon and Netflix. Of the terrestrial channels, US corporation Viacom owns Channel 5, while BBC and Channel 4 are public service broadcasters.

As the state funded broadcaster, the BBC has major influence, but its 'neutrality' stance often appears to be little more than an affirmation of the status quo. As Peter Oborne points out, lies are consistently fed to 'journalists' and then reported as facts without any checks taking place. The political connections and sympathies of past and present news and current affairs employees are evident in their pre and post BBC careers.

Social media is dominated by Facebook and Twitter, with the former playing host to adverts from shadow groups, as Jess Smee reported in *The rising clout of digital media and the UK election*. In 2019, the Conservative Party went further and paid for search engine adverts that directed people to bogus websites purporting to be related to the Labour Party. During a leadership debate between Jeremy Corbyn and Alexander Boris de Pfeffel Johnson, the Party also redesigned its twitter page so that it appeared to be a 'fact-checking' site.

Digital strategies have also been used to target individuals with misleading information and adverts from surreptitious sources, as in the notorious case of Cambridge Analytica. Covert surveillance and sharing of online activities, for example, are used to influence political behaviour. Information gathered in this way and from bogus on-line surveys, is subjected to psychometric analyses to predict political persuasions and help parties target individuals with messages designed to resonate with their point of view.

Money

Tressell

The other characters ridicule Owen's view that 'money is the cause of poverty,' believing instead that it is the absence of money. They are also incredulous at the suggestion that: '... money is in itself of no value and of no real use whatever.'

In Chapter 25, the following argument is made to support this assertion:

> 'A man might possess so much money that, in England, he would be comparatively rich, and yet if he went to some country where the cost of living is very high he would find himself in a condition of poverty. Or one might conceivably be in a place where the necessaries of life could not be bought for money at all. Therefore it is more conducive to an intelligent understanding of the subject if we say that to be rich consists not necessarily in having much money, but in being able to enjoy an abundance of the things that are made by work; and that poverty consists not merely in being without money, but in being short of the necessaries and comforts of life - or in other words in being short of the Benefits of Civilization, the things that are all, without exception, produced by work.'

Later in the same Chapter, the point is developed in response to the charge that socialism is about 'sharing out:'

> 'Supposing all the money was shared out equally; and suppose there was enough of it for everyone to have ten thousand pounds; and suppose they then all thought they were rich and none of them would work. What would they live on? Their money? Could they eat it or drink it or wear it? It wouldn't take them very long to find out that this wonderful money - which under the present system is the most powerful thing in existence - is really of no more use than so much dirt. They would speedily perish, not from lack of money, but from lack of wealth - that is, from lack of things that are made by work.'

Further on:

> '... it's money that's caused all these people to lose sight of the true purpose of labour - the production of the things we need? All these people are suffering from the delusion that it doesn't matter what kind of work they do - or whether they merely do nothing - so long as they get MONEY for doing it. Under the present extraordinary system, that's the only object they have in view - to get money.'

This point is put another way in Chapter 45, as proof that money is the CAUSE OF POVERTY:

> '... under present conditions no work can be done without money; and so we have the spectacle of a great army of people compelled to stand idle and starve by the side of the raw materials from which their labour could produce abundance of all the things they need - they are rendered helpless by the power of Money! Those who possess all the money say that the necessaries of life shall not be produced except for their profit.'

Later in the chapter, during his 'Great Oration' Barrington alludes to another consequence:

> 'Under the present system men intrigue for and obtain or are pitchforked into positions for which they have no natural ability at all; the only reason they desire these positions is because of the salaries attached to them. These fellows get the money and the work is done by underpaid subordinates whom the world never hears of.'

This also means that:

> '... there are men at the head of affairs whose only object is the accumulation of money.'

Their lust for money has other benefits, however, such as its power to purchase 'Honour and Praise:'

> 'Some of them spend thousands of pounds for the honour of being able to write "MP" after their names. Others buy titles. Others pay huge sums to gain admission to exclusive circles of society.'

It is worth remembering, that the system Tressell was referring to at the time was known as the 'Gold Standard.' Hence Barrington's remark:

> 'If the Government of a country began to issue large amounts of paper money under the present system, it would inevitably lead to bankruptcy, for the simple reason that paper money under the present system - bank-notes, bank drafts, postal orders, cheques or any other form - is merely a printed promise to pay the amount - in gold or silver - on demand or at a certain date. Under the present system if a Government issues more paper money than it possesses gold and silver to redeem, it is of course bankrupt.'

21st Century

The fixation with money continues unabated; albeit with some new characteristics. This is due, in part, to the social and purchasing power it offers to those who possess it in large quantities, but the obverse is also evident in the lives of people burdened with rent, mortgage, student loans and other forms of domestic DEBT.

Added to this, a miasma of public perception is created and maintained by governments, corporations and their MEDIA outlets. From the cost of living to the cost of government spending and borrowing everything is expressed and measured in monetary terms. The same agencies also exhibit a preoccupation with profit-making activities that use money to make more money, such as speculation in stocks, bonds, currencies and financial instruments. Likewise, the privatization of health, social care and welfare provision, means that the quality and effectiveness of these services are equated with cost, price and value for money, instead of outcomes for claimants, patients, tenants and other service users.

In and of itself, the coins, notes and symbols that pass for money, still have little or no intrinsic value. Since 1973, there is no longer a connection between currencies and the price of gold. A system of fiat monies (Latin: 'let it be done') is now the order of the day, the validity of which rests on the authority of central banks like the US federal Reserve, the Bank of England and the European Central Bank. For nations that issue and control their own medium of exchange, therefore, there is no longer any prospect of them going bankrupt, as evidenced by the vast amounts of 'new' money created by central banks to bail out financial institutions in response to financial crises in the 2000s.

An uncritical acceptance of this reality has produced some eccentric proposals designed to remedy failings of the current system and thereby guarantee its continuation. One such example is the so-called Modern Monetary Theory, which proposes that national governments fund public spending by creating new money, instead of borrowing. While this might free nation states from the power of speculators and rating agencies, it merely follows Keynes' solutions to low investor confidence and consumer spending as noted by Simon Wren-Lewis, *Labour's Fiscal Credibility Rule in Context*. What it does not do, is address the causes of HOMELESSNESS, POVERTY, wage-labour etc.

The same charge can be made against the idea of a Universal Basic Income. Even worse, is its potential to reinforce the social power of money, through the allocation of a basic income from which individuals would be required to purchase education, health, social care and other welfare provision from profit seeking corporations. Neither would either of these nostrums negate the confusion of salary size with importance and capability, when in reality 'the work is done by underpaid subordinates.'

In its *Executive pay in the FTSE 100 - 2019 review*, for example, the Chartered Institute of Personnel and Development records the following:

- Chief Executive pay is 117 times that of the average worker;
- In 2018, the average annual pay for chief executives was £3.46 million; and,
- The same chief executives would have to work for three days – 2nd January 2020 to 17.00 6th January – or 33 hours, to be paid the same amount as the average full-time worker would receive for the whole of 2020.

Monopoly

Tressell

The practice whereby one producer or trader has the sole right to deal in a particular commodity, is identified by Owen in Chapter 15 as a CAUSE OF POVERTY:

> 'It's caused by Private Monopoly. That is the present system. They have monopolized everything that it is possible to monopolize; they have got the whole earth, the minerals in the earth and the streams that water the earth.'

Mr Amos Grinder is given as an example in Chapter 20, where it is said that he:

> '...had practically monopolized the greengrocery trade and now owned nearly all the fruiterers' shops in the town. As for the other shops, if they did not buy their stocks from him - or, rather, the company of which he was managing director and principal shareholder - if these other fruiterers and greengrocers did not buy their stuff from his company, he tried to smash them by opening branches in their immediate neighbourhood and selling below cost.'

Finally, in Chapter 45 Barrington implies that the process is an almost inevitable consequence of:

> '... the efficient organization of industry by the trusts that control and are beginning to monopolize production.'

21st Century

Supermarkets like Tesco and Sainsbury's function in a similar fashion to Amos Grinder, with the former running nearly 3,000 Express, One Stop and Metro convenience outlets. They operate by buying out local butchers, fishmongers and other retailers - often anonymously through third parties - and open their local variant to keep the area free of competition. At the other end of the supply chain, the size of their market share allows them to dictate terms to farmers and small-scale producers and manufacturers of food and other commodities.

Behind the façade of the shopfront, the branding of products is designed to create an illusion of choice and customer loyalty in order to control demand. Companies like Proctor and Gamble, and Unilever, for example, are responsible for many high-street products. The same is true in other fields of production, including car giants like Volkswagen and General Motors. All of which serves to conceal who actually owns and controls the businesses that produce the things people buy and the ways in which they are delivered and offered for sale.

Piece-Work

Tressell

A particular kind of exploitative practice utilized by the employers of Mugsborough was payment according to the amount of work done. The method is first introduced in Chapter 20 in relation to women who work at home:

> 'The blouses were paid for at the rate of from two shillings to five shillings a dozen, the women having to provide their own machine and cotton, besides calling for and delivering the work. These poor women were able to clear from six to eight shillings a week: and to earn even that they had to work almost incessantly for fourteen or sixteen hours a day.'

Jack Linden's daughter-in-law is recorded as making blouses and pinafores in this fashion for Sweater & Co. in Chapter 33, but what these descriptions omit to mention, is the fact that homeworkers also have to pay for heating and lighting.

Other examples include "The Hook and Eye Carders" included in Bert White's Pandorama, Chapter 29:

> '... the inside of a room in Slumtown, with a mother and three children and the old grandmother sewin' hooks and eyes on cards to be sold in drapers' shops. It ses

> underneath the pitcher that 384 hooks and 384 eyes has to be joined together and sewed on cards for one penny.'

In Chapter 35, the Reverend Habbakuk Bosher also employed the method for charitable purposes in his 'Labour Yard,' where the unemployed were put to work:

> 'A log of wood about the size of a railway sleeper had to be sawn into twelve pieces, and each of these had to be chopped into four. For sawing and chopping one log in this manner the worker was paid ninepence. One log made two bags of firewood, which were sold for a shilling each - a trifle under the usual price. The men who delivered the bags were paid three half-pence for each two bags.'

Another example involved the religious character known as Slyme who, in Chapter 21 is paid according to the number of rolls of paper he uses when decorating a room, and is caught in the acting of destroying rolls in order to increase his income.

21st **Century**

People doing piece work are now expected to be paid a 'fair rate' for each task or piece of work completed, which is equivalent to 120% of the National Minimum Wage and based on the time it would take an average worker to complete each task. There are, however, grey areas.

Self-employed couriers used by companies like Amazon and Hermes, for example, are allocated a number of parcels to deliver in an estimated time period. This estimate is not fixed, however, because couriers can work to their own schedule and earn more MONEY by delivering more parcels.

Equally ambiguous are homeworking arrangements, such as mystery shopping, product testing, focus group participation, survey completion, transcription and freelance writing. The isolated nature of the work-place can make it difficult for co-ordination and organization amongst workers, and the precarious nature of contracts means there are risks in challenging employers. Problems may also be encountered if payment is refused because the standard of work is not considered to be acceptable.

Although not immediately obvious, piece rates are also paid in addition to a basic salary that is calculated according to hours worked. These can take different forms, but include informal tips given to workers employed in hospitality, as well as bonuses or commission paid per call or sale completed.

Politics

Tressell

Even though the Parliamentary election in Mugsborough is cast as a binary choice between Liberal and Tory, Tressell and his mouthpiece Owen, are scathing about working class support for either party.

As the narrator observes in Chapter 44:

> '... it was not until the topic of Parliamentary elections was mentioned that evidence of their insanity was forthcoming. It then almost invariably appeared that they were subject to the most extraordinary hallucinations and extravagant delusions, the commonest being that the best thing that the working people could do to bring about an improvement in their condition, was to continue to elect their Liberal and Tory employers to make laws for and to rule over them! At such times, if anyone ventured to point out to them that that was what they had been doing all their lives, and referred them to the manifold evidences that met them wherever they turned their eyes of its folly and futility, they were generally immediately seized with a paroxysm of the most furious mania,

and were with difficulty prevented from savagely assaulting those who differed from them.

Earlier, in Chapter 29, Bert White describes things in similar terms:

> 'Our next scene is called "The Rival Candidates, or, a Scene during the General Election". On the left you will observe, standin' up in a motor car, a swell bloke with a eyeglass stuck in one eye, and a overcoat with a big fur collar and cuffs, addressing the crowd: this is the Honourable Augustus Slumrent, the Conservative candidate. On the other side of the road we see another motor car and another swell bloke with a round pane of glass in one eye and a overcoat with a big fur collar and cuffs, standing up in the car and addressin' the crowd. This is Mr Mandriver, the Liberal candidate. The crowds of shabby-lookin' chaps standin' round the motor cars wavin' their 'ats and cheerin' is workin' men. Both the candidates is tellin' 'em the same old story, and each of 'em is askin' the workin' men to elect 'im to Parlimint, and promisin' to do something or other to make things better for the lower horders."

Meanwhile, Chapter 48 tells how back in Mugsborough 'The ragged-trousered Tory workmen:'

> '... stuck election cards bearing Sir Graball's photograph in their windows and tied bits of blue and yellow ribbon - Sir Graball's colours - on their underfed children.'

Liberal supporters did likewise. While:

> 'The town was soon deluged with mendacious literature and smothered with huge posters ... "Vote for Sweater - Free Trade and Cheap Food." or "Vote for D'Encloseland: Tariff Reform and Plenty of Work!'

Other forms of propaganda are also described:

> 'There was one Tory poster that represented the interior of a public house; in front of the bar, with a quart pot in his hand, a clay pipe in his mouth, and a load of tools on his back, stood a degraded-looking brute who represented the Tory ideal of what an Englishman should be; the letterpress on the poster said it was a man! This is the ideal of manhood that they hold up to the majority of their fellow countrymen, but privately- amongst themselves - the Tory aristocrats regard such 'men' with far less respect than they do the lower animals.

> 'The Liberal posters were not quite so offensive. They were more cunning, more specious, more hypocritical and consequently more calculated to mislead and deceive the more intelligent of the voters.'

Ignorance is one of the reasons given in the opening Chapter, to explain the behaviour of inhabitants of Mugsborough:

> 'Some of them were under the delusion that they were Conservatives: similarly, others imagined themselves to be Liberals. As a matter of fact, most of them were nothing. They knew as much about the public affairs of their own country as they did of the condition of affairs in the planet of Jupiter.'

They often admit as much, like Crass in Chapter One: 'I don't never worry my 'ed about politics.' and Easton: 'Well, I don't go in for politics much, either, ...' Philpot also expresses a similar sentiment, while taking a more sanguine view:

> 'There ain't no use in the likes of us trubblin our 'eds or quarrelin about politics. It don't make a dam bit of difference who you votes for or who gets in. They're hall the same; workin the horicle for their own benefit ... It's no use worrying.'

In Chapter 15, the man on the pail adds his view:

> 'Wot the 'ell's the use of the likes of us troublin' our 'eads about politics?'

For Owen in the opening chapter, however, the response is one of complete and utter exasperation and disdain:

> 'A little while ago you made the remark that you never trouble yourself about what you call politics, and some of the rest agreed with you that to do so is not worth while. Well, since you never "worry" yourself about these things, it follows that you know nothing about them; yet you do not hesitate to express the most decided opinions concerning matters of which you admittedly know nothing. Presently, when there is an election, you will go and vote in favour of a policy of which you know nothing. I say that since you never take the trouble to find out which side is right or wrong you have no right to express any opinion. You are not fit to vote. You should not be allowed to vote.'

21st Century

If the legitimacy of the results of the 2019 British General Election are to be taken at face value, it seems that some voters were suffering from hallucinations and delusions similar to those described by Tressell.

Constituencies like Bishop Auckland, Blyth Valley, Bolsover, Durham North West, Leigh and Redcar all elected Conservative Party representatives, despite their past experience of Tory rule.

It is difficult to gauge apathy and reasons why people voted the way they did, but an Ipsos MORI report *How Britain voted in the 2019 election* provides some evidence that the Conservatives increased their vote share by 3% in the following categories: skilled manual workers; Semi-skilled and unskilled manual workers; people in receipt of a State pension who do not work, casual workers and unemployed people receiving benefits. In the category of Labour Leave voters, it is also estimated that only 65% stayed loyal to Labour, while 23% actually voted Conservative.

Albeit a caricature concocted by 'Onward' a Tory Party interest group, this data is suggestive of the 'Workington Man' who is said to be older, white, northern English, a non-graduate and a Leave voter. It also plays into the narrative surrounding the 'Blue-Collar Conservatism' project. Behind the mask, however, there lies another caricature as demonstrated by the wording of a 2014 Conservative poster which exclaimed:

BINGO!

Cutting the Bingo Tax and Beer Duty

To help hardworking people do

More of the things they enjoy

Mendacious literature still abounds. Take the charges made against the Liberal Democrats in 2019, for example, of using bar charts that were misleading. Leaflets that proclaimed 'only the Lib Dems can beat the Tories,' were alleged to have made selective use of European and local election results to conflate outcomes and constituencies. Likewise, party polling was presented as objective, but relied on skewed questions like: "Imagine that the result in your constituency was expected to be very close between the Conservative and the Liberal Democrat candidate, and none of the other parties were competitive. In this scenario, which party would you vote for?" These and more examples are documented by The Coalition for Reform in Political Advertising in their report: *Illegal, Indecent, Dishonest & Untruthful.*

Poverty

Tressell

In contrast to the other characters' simple identification of poverty with a lack of MONEY, Owen offers a more nuanced interpretation in Chapter One:

> 'What I call poverty is when people are not able to secure for themselves all the benefits of civilization; the necessaries, comforts, pleasures and refinements of life, leisure, books, theatres, pictures, music, holidays, travel, good and beautiful homes, good clothes, good and pleasant food.'

> 'If a man is only able to provide himself and his family with the bare necessaries of existence, that man's family is living in poverty.'

The theme is repeated in Chapter Seven:

> 'Poverty ... consists in a shortage of the necessaries of life. When those things are so scarce or so dear that people are unable to obtain sufficient of them to satisfy all their needs, those people are in a condition of poverty.'

And again, in Chapter 25:

> 'Poverty ... consists in a shortage of the necessaries of life - or rather, of the benefits of civilization.'

He also makes a distinction between poverty and destitution in Chapter Seven:

> 'In my opinion, we are all in a state of poverty even when we have employment - the condition we are reduced to when we're out of work is more properly described as destitution.'

> '... we might have "Plenty of Work" and yet be in a state of destitution.'

The numbers affected are quantified by Bert White in Chapter 29:

> 'Thirteen millions of people in England always on the verge of starvation.'

And again, by Barrington in Chapter 45:

> 'It is an admitted fact that about thirteen millions of our people are always on the verge of starvation.'

Who also recounts the effects:

> 'The significant results of this poverty face us on every side. The alarming and persistent increase of insanity. The large number of would-be recruits for the army who have to be rejected because they are physically unfit; ... More than one-third of the children of the working classes in London have some sort of mental or physical defect; defects in development;

> defects of eyesight; abnormal nervousness; rickets, and mental dullness.'

In response to the charge that money is wasted on education, here responds:

> 'What can be more brutal and senseless than trying to "educate" a poor little, hungry, ill-clad child?'

This last point had already been alluded to by the narrator in Chapter 37:

> '... it was a matter of common knowledge that the majority of the children attending the local elementary schools were insufficiently fed.'

21st Century

The Joseph Rowntree Foundation Report *UK Poverty 2018* defines poverty as an income of less than 60% of median income after housing costs, income tax, National Insurance and Council Tax payments, contributions to occupational pension schemes, maintenance payments and student loan repayments. In other words, it is a measure of relative poverty which includes:

~ 8.2 million working-age adults,
~ 4.1 million children
~ 1.9 million pensioners.

These figures can be broken down further to show that:

- eight million people in poverty live in a family where at least one person is working.
- 1.5 million people were living in destitution at some point during 2017, including 365,000 children.
- 4.6 million people live in persistent poverty.

To put these figures into context, these levels of poverty exist in an economy which, according to the International Monetary Fund's *World Economic Outlook October 2019*, is ranked as the sixth-largest in terms of Gross Domestic Product.

In broader terms, the 2017, Child Poverty (Scotland) Act, provides the following categories:

- Relative Poverty - households with income below 60% of the UK median after housing costs
- Absolute Poverty - households with income below 60% of the 2010/11 median
- Low Income and Material Deprivation - households with income below 70% of the median and without access to a number of goods or services
- Persistent Poverty – those living in relative poverty in three out of the last four years

An Institute for Fiscal Studies report *Living standards, poverty and inequality in the UK: 2019* also offers a definition of severe poverty, based on three criteria:

- Very low household income - below 50% or 40% of the median,
- Low household expenditure - not being able to afford basic items
- Material Deprivation – not able to keep the home warm or save each month.

It also equates destitution with HOMELESSNESS and malnutrition.

Suicide

Tressell

Perhaps the most morbid aspect of the tale is its references to 'Domestic Tragedy.' The subject is alluded to in the opening Chapter:

> '... a yet smaller but still very great number actually died of hunger, or, maddened by privation, killed themselves and their children in order to put a period to their misery.'

In Chapter Four, the topic is re-introduced with reference to a placard outside a newsagent's shop and resumes in Chapter 6, when Owen is confronted with the headlines of the newspaper he bought at the shop: 'Terrible Domestic Tragedy'.

Some of the details are narrated:

> 'It was one of the ordinary poverty crimes. The man had been without employment for many weeks and they had been living by pawning or selling their furniture and other possessions. ... When the police entered the house, they found, in one of the upper rooms, the dead bodies of the woman and the two children ...
>
> 'There was no bedstead and no furniture in the room except the straw mattress and the

ragged clothes and blankets which formed the bed upon the floor.

'The man's body was found in the kitchen...

'No particle of food was found in the house, and on a nail in the wall in the kitchen was hung a piece of blood-smeared paper on which was written in pencil:

"This is not my crime, but society's."'

In the following paragraphs Owen considers the best method for accomplishing the same task, should his situation become so desperate, noting:

'... that most of these killings were done in more or less the same crude, cruel messy way.'

Harlow also provides another example in Chapter 15:

'... the case of a family whose house got into such a condition that the landlord had given them notice and the father had committed suicide because the painters had come to turn 'em out of house and home.'

Owen returns to the topic in Chapter 23:

'He thought of the man who had killed his wife and children. The jury had returned the usual verdict, 'Temporary Insanity'. It never seemed to occur to these people that the truth was that to continue to suffer hopelessly like this was evidence of permanent insanity.'

21st Century

A 2017 Samaritans' summary report, *Dying from Inequality*, sets out the following as key facts:

~ Areas of higher socioeconomic deprivation have higher rates of suicide.
~ The adverse effects of economic recession make men more at risk of suicide.
~ The unemployed are more at risk of dying by suicide than those in work.
~ Increases in suicide rates are linked to economic recessions.
~ Greater levels of deprivation for individuals, mean a higher risk of suicidal behaviour.

In other words, low incomes, job insecurity, zero-hours contracts, unmanageable DEBT and poor housing are all indicators of suicide risk.

There are also a number of suicides that are linked by coroners to the activities of the Department for Work and Pensions (DWP). The DWP refuses to disclose these figures, but a study published in the April, 2016 issue of the Journal of Epidemiology and Community Health - *'First, do no harm': are disability assessments associated with adverse trends in mental health?* - found that the Department's work capability reassessment process was associated with an extra 590 suicides. These figures only apply to

England for the years 2010 - 2013 and are equated to 5% of the total number of suicides.

In February 2020, an interim report by the National Audit Office *Information held by the Department for Work & Pensions on deaths by suicide of benefit claimants* found that the DWP had investigated 69 suicides of benefit claimants since 2014-15. It added that it is highly unlikely that number represents the number of cases it could have investigated in the past six years.

Unnecessary Work

Tressell

During his attempt to demonstrate the real CAUSE OF POVERTY in Chapter 25, Owen defines unnecessary work as:

> '... producing things or doing things which - though useful and necessary to the Imbecile System - cannot be described as the necessaries of life or the benefits of civilization.'

He then categorizes the following occupations as unnecessary:

> '... Commercial Travellers, Canvassers, Insurance agents, commission agents, the great number of Shop Assistants, the majority of clerks, workmen employed in the construction and adornment of business premises, people occupied with what they call "Business", which means being very busy without producing anything. Then there is a vast army of people engaged in designing, composing, painting or printing advertisements, things which are for the most part of no utility whatever, the object of most advertisements is merely to persuade people to buy from one firm rather than from another.'

Later adding:

> '... they are all very busy - working very hard - but to all useful intents and purposes they are doing Nothing.'

By way of contrast, necessary, rational or useful work is said to involve:

> '... the production of the benefits of civilization - the necessaries, refinements and comforts of life.'

21st Century

Although it is not possible to draw a precise comparison between the 'unnecessary' occupations listed above, the Office for National Statistics last published an annual snapshot of employment by occupation for the period April – June 2018. The following categories and figures are taken from that Emp04 dataset. They are not definitive, in as much as some similar functions might exist under a 'rational' system. In this example, however, 6,370,000 or 20% of those in work are: 'people occupied with what they call "Business."'

Managers, Directors and Senior Officials

Marketing & sales directors	227,000
Advertising & public relations directors	42,000
Financial Institution Managers & Directors	91,000
Managers & Directors in Retail & Wholesale	336,000
Property, housing & estate managers	167,000
Shopkeepers & proprietors (wholesale & retail)	120,000
Total:	983,000

Business, Research & Administrative Professionals
Chartered & certified accountants	182,000
Management consultants & business analysts	175,000
Business & financial project management	266,000
Actuaries, economists & statisticians	48,000
Business & related research	45,000
Other business, research & administrative	<u>53,000</u>
Total:	769,000

Business, Finance and Related Associate Professionals
Estimators, valuers & assessors	61,000
Brokers	53,000
Insurance underwriters	34,000
Finance & investment analysts & advisers	203,000
Taxation experts	34,000
Importers & exporters	8,000
Financial & accounting technicians	16,000
Financial accounts managers	177,000
Other business & related associate professionals	<u>178,000</u>
Total:	764,000

Sales, Marketing & Related Associate Professionals
Buyers & procurement officers	55,000
Business sales executives	119,000
Marketing associate professionals	211,000
Estate agents & auctioneers	51,000
Sales accounts & business development managers	459,000
Conference & exhibition managers and organisers	<u>82,000</u>
Total:	977,000

Administrative Occupations: Finance
Credit controllers	36,000
Book-keepers, payroll managers & wages clerks	434,000
Bank & post office clerks	106,000
Finance officers	43,000
Other financial administrative occupations	<u>165,000</u>
Total:	784,000

Administrative Occupations: Records
Pensions & insurance clerks & assistants 75,000
Other Administrative Occupations
Sales administrators 76,000
Sales Assistants & Retail Cashiers
Sales & retail assistants 1,079,000
Retail cashiers & check-out operators 200,000
Telephone salespersons 25,000
Pharmacy & other dispensing assistants 80,000
Vehicle & parts salespersons & advisers <u>43,000</u>
Total: 1,427,000

Sales Related Occupations
Collector salespersons & credit agents 11,000
Debt, rent & other cash collectors 30,000
Roundspersons & van salespersons 29,000
Market & street traders & assistants 19,000
Merchandisers&window dressers 29,000
Other sales related occupations <u>52,000</u>
Total: 170,000

Sales Supervisors 201,000

Elementary Sales Occupations 144,000

Welfare

Tressell

Barrington's mention of 'miserable Old Age Pensions,' during his 'Great Oration' in Chapter 45, seems to reference the Liberal Government's Old-Age Pensions Act 1908. The provision of which were indeed miserable. Only people aged over 70 were eligible, and only if they had worked to their 'full potential' and even then, they were means-tested. In Mugsborough, what counted as 'relief of distress' was equally meagre and hard to obtain.

That was the function of the Organized Benevolence Society which, as described in Chapter 36, oversaw the allocation of '... tickets of admission to hospitals, convalescent homes and dispensaries ...' and '... for soup or orders for shillingsworths of groceries or coal.'

Mary Linden is one such example, recounted in Chapter 33:

> 'A lady district visitor who called occasionally sometimes gave Mary an order for a hundredweight of coal or a shillingsworth of groceries, or a ticket for a quart of soup, which Elsie fetched in the evening from the Soup Kitchen. But this was not very often, because, as the lady said, there were so many cases similar to

theirs that it was impossible to do more than a very little for any one of them. '

Another source of 'relief' receives attention in the same chapter and again it involved the Linden family:

> '... the relieving officer, who took him before the Board, who did not think it a suitable case for out-relief, and after some preliminaries it was arranged that Linden and his wife were to go into the workhouse, and Mary was to be allowed three shillings a week to help her to support herself and the two children.'

Aspects of the Poor Law system are illustrated further in Chapter 28, where the Guardians end up imprisoning a man and supporting his family because they cannot afford to pay his required contribution:

> 'Newman ... had been arrested and sentenced to a month's imprisonment because he had not been able to pay his poor rates, and the Board of Guardians were allowing his wife three shillings a week to maintain herself and the three children.'

At least some people benefited from the Organized Benefit Society, as explained in Chapter 35:

> 'They never gave the 'case' the money. The ticket system serves three purposes. It prevents the 'case' abusing the 'charity' by

> spending the money on drink. It advertises the benevolence of the donors: and it enables the grocer ... to get rid of any stale or damaged stock he may have on hand.'

Nepotism is never far away:

> 'Then there was the Soup Kitchen ... The man who ran this was a relative of the secretary of the OBS. He cadged all the ingredients for the soup from different tradespeople ... Well-intentioned, charitable old women with more money than sense sent him donations in cash, and he sold the soup for a penny a basin - or a penny a quart to those who brought jugs.'

In Chapter 37, we are told 'Another specious fraud was the "Distress Committee," [which] ... was supposed to exist for the purpose of providing employment for 'deserving cases'". To decide if they were 'deserving,' each applicant was confronted with:

> '... a 'Record Paper', three pages of it were covered with insulting, inquisitive, irrelevant questions concerning the private affairs and past life of the 'case' who wished to be permitted to work for his living, and all these had to be answered ...'

Later, in the penultimate chapter, we learn of:

> '... a new and better way, calculated to keep down the number of applicants. The result

of this innovation was that no more forms were issued, but the applicants for work were admitted into the office one at a time, and were there examined by a junior clerk, somewhat after the manner of a French Juge d'Instruction interrogating a criminal, the clerk filling in the form according to the replies of the culprit.'

21st Century

By and large, the state of welfare in Britain is the product of two acts of parliament. The Welfare Reform Act 2012 introduced: Universal Credit, a 'claimant commitment,' Personal Independence Payments, the 'bedroom tax,' the 'benefit cap,' benefit sanctions, and reformed Employment and Support Allowance. This was followed in 2016 by the Welfare Reform and Work Act, the provisions of which, included: a freeze on social security benefits and tax credits for four years, a maximum of two children for families claiming benefit, reduced the benefit cap from £20,000 or £13,400 for families and individuals respectively (£23,000 and £15,410 for Greater London), and replaced Mortgage Interest Relief with an interest bearing loan.

A variety of forms have also been designed to evaluate whether applicants are deserving cases, including:

~ ESA1 for Income-related or Contribution-based Employment Support Allowance - 64 pages

- ESA50 Capability for work questionnaire - 25 pages
- NSESAF1 for 'New Style' Employment and Support Allowance - 22 pages
- UC50 a Universal Credit capability for work questionnaire - 24 pages
- PIP1 Personal Independence Payments claim form - 20 pages
- PIP2 Personal Independence Payments form 'How your disability Affects you' - 33 pages
- AR1 and PIP.1043 Award Review forms - 16 pages

For Universal Credit, however, applications have to be made online, whether a person has internet access or not.

Once these obstacles have been negotiated, claimants face a series of interviews with a 'work coach' to monitor attempts to find work, assess if illness or disability affects ability to work, and require people to sign a 'Claimant Commitment'. For Work Capability Assessments and Award Reviews, claimants are required to attend a face-to-face meeting with a private company 'health professional' who completes a questionnaire according to their interpretation of the answers given.

People who fall foul of this regime can have their support stopped permanently or temporarily, as outlined in the 2013 Press Release *Benefit sanctions – ending the 'something for nothing' culture*. The title of which sums up the attitude toward people who are poor, ill, elderly and disabled.

The last resort for people who have been refused benefit, have had their claim delayed or cannot live on the amount awarded, is the Food Bank (see CHARITY). Even here, however, there is a voucher system whereby doctors, health visitors, social workers, Citizens Advice or other authorized bodies make referrals. Having overcome the stigma of requesting help, the person has to provide information that helps officials to 'identify the cause of the crisis, offer practical guidance' and provide a dole of food. Much of these provisions are donated by the general public, who have bought them from supermarkets that display their philanthropy by providing collection points for goods that have been bought in store and therefore provide a profit for the retailer.

Conclusion

The aim of this book is to ask and answer the following questions: are the circumstances described in *The Ragged Trousered Philanthropists* still true and, if so, how and why? Anyone who has read at least one of the chapters should be able to answer the first two questions and, if the answer is affirmative, add examples to those given.

The task that remains, is to explain why it is so and to say what can be done about it.

Covering the period from 1870 to 1914, La Belle Époque is synonymous with the Golden Age in North America and the latter years of Pax Britannica. For the simplistic historian these years represent an age of optimism, peace, prosperity, technological and scientific progress. Beneath the surface, however, the reality is very different, meaning that the period is more fittingly described as a Gilded Age, whereby the veneer of prosperity masked underlying poverty, inequality and squalor – as depicted in Tressell's description of Macaroni's Royal Italian Café. This was followed by the 'roaring 20s' when post-war reconstruction was equated with prosperity.

As noted in the Introduction, a similar façade can be found in descriptions of Britain after World War Two, as an era of dramatically rising standards of living and a so-called compromise between Capital and Labour. Then, in numerous speeches from 1997 to 2007, Gordon Brown as Chancellor of the Exchequer heralded the 'end of boom and bust.' His tenuous grasp of history and, for that matter, political economy was, however, laid bare in his Pre-Budget Statement delivered to Parliament on 25th November, 1997:

> 'For 40 years our economy has an unenviable history, under governments of both parties, of boom and bust.'

If everything in the garden was so rosy, it might be wondered why it was necessary to introduce what has become known as the welfare state. Of course, the Poor Law had been in operation since 1601:

> '... for setting to work all such persons married or unmarried, having no means to maintain them, or no ordinary and daily trade of life to get their living by, and also to raise ... competent sums of money, for, and towards the necessary relief of the lame, impotent, old, blind, and such other among them being poor, and not able to work.'

It was reformed in 1834, in response to the Speenhamland System that subsidised low wages from local rates, but not abolished until 1948.

Liberal Reforms at the start of the 20th Century are often misrepresented as the origins of the Welfare State, but in reality, they built on measures introduced by the previous Conservative administration. A major factor, was the fear that undernourishment and illness jeopardized imperial military control, as 40% of recruits were unfit for service in the second Boer War due to poverty-related illnesses. As was the introduction of 'meagre' old age pension in an attempt ease pressure on work-houses.

Even the 'five giants' identified by the academic and later Liberal MP and peer William Beveridge are considered to be worthy of little more than ameliorative tampering. All that is needed to address:

Want	is an <u>adequate</u> <u>income</u>.
Disease	is <u>access</u> to health
Ignorance	is educational <u>opportunity</u>
Squalor	is <u>adequate</u> housing
Idleness	is <u>gainful employment</u>

In the 21st Century this translates into tax credits that top up low wages, housing benefit that profits private sector landlords and a form of workfare, that requires the unemployed to take any job offered regardless of suitability or location or lose entitlement to allowances.

Next comes the agenda of Welfare Reform and austerity which used the financial crisis of 2008 as an excuse to return to Poor Law principles in everything but name. This involved a shift in the definition of poverty and its causes away from income to: family breakdown; educational failure; welfare dependency; worklessness; addiction to drugs and alcohol; and personal debt. In other words, it moves responsibility to the victim, over the socio-economic system.

Responsibility for the social and economic effects of government policies was even exported to the European Union, through a masterful slight-of-hand that weaved free trade, migration and fiscal policy into the web of deceit. Somehow the impression was given that the Cabinet and Parliament were forced to adopt a policy of austerity due to payments made to the European Union and that government taxation and spending plans would be liberated once Britain had left.

Free trade was also played as a panacea, that ignored its historical role. Such as the 19th Century campaigns for and against the Corn Laws, which personified the differences between landed interests and economic liberals and contributed to the formation of Conservative and Liberal parties. In the 1920s Stanley Baldwin committed the Conservative Party to protection, thereby casting the Liberal Party as supporters of Free trade.

Post-World War Two the General Agreement on Tariffs and Trade proposed a progressive lowering of barriers, reduction in tariffs and discrimination – such as the British Imperial Preference - with the ultimate goal of world free trade to be achieved via negotiation. With effect from 1st January 1995, negotiations have been overseen by the World Trade Organization, whose terms are also touted as a substitute for a trade agreement with the European Union although this would involve some tariffs.

The policies of economic liberalism now extolled by the Conservative Party and its fellow-travellers are therefore in contrast to the party's earlier incarnations. Their prophecies of prosperity for all in a neo-liberal idyll are also in direct contradiction with the experience of conservative governments' performance since the 1980s. So too, the Janus like claim to be looking forward to a brighter future, while harking back to an imaginary 19th century paradise.

So, what is happening here? Is it that wilful ignorance condemns people to repeat the mistakes of the past? Is it rational to try the same solutions over and over again in the hope of achieving a different result? The answers to these questions is yes and no, because as Frank Owen remarks in Chapter 15:

> 'There are many causes, but they are all part of and inseparable from the system. In order to do away with poverty we must destroy the causes: to do away with the causes we must destroy the whole system.'

In order to achieve this, however, the productive forces of existing society must have been exhausted, and the material bases of the new nurtured to fruition. Which leads on neatly to the questions of mechanization, automation and artificial intelligence.

The drive to replace human labour-power with machines has an inexorable logic: reduce costs, increase productivity and maximise profits. As a number of writers have pointed out, however, areas of production are now approaching a point where machines can replicate themselves and therefore produce with minimal or no human input at all. This presents two challenges to the existing mode of production: what happens to people who are no longer needed to produce commodities; and, who will buy the products if no-one works to earn money.

Mason raises these points in *Postcapitalism* but also addresses the potential of computers to replace market mechanisms as a way of calculating the production and allocation of resources. Thus on page 226 he states:

> '... we need to revisit the calculation debate for a reason that should be obvious: technology is eroding the price mechanism without the parallel rise of a planned economy.'

Writing in 2014, however, he was unable to take into account the predictive nature of artificial intelligence uncovered by Zuboff.

Likewise, the development of the 'smart-home' and Nest technology that gather and process data on domestic use and therefore demand. All this information can and is being used by producers, but not for the benefit of consumers. More importantly, it offers the potential to replace market mechanisms with a democratically controlled planning process. In which people liberated from the necessity of wage-labour are free to participate.

Finally, the example of Amazon Go discussed on page 55 of this book, offers a means by which people can access the everyday products they need, without money, price and therefore the process of exchange governing transactions. None of these possibilities are written in stone, but their existence offers the opportunity to exploit the contradictions between automation, wage-labour and commodity production for sale to transcend and transform existing social relations.

Further Reading

Cited in text

Association of Chief Executives of Voluntary Organisations, *Pay and Equalities Survey 2019*,
https://www.acevo.org.uk/publications/pay-and-equalities-survey-2019/
Last visited 24.2.20

Abel Smith, Brian and Townsend, Peter, (1965) *The Poor and the Poorest* (G Bell & Sons)

Affordable Housing Commission (June, 2019) *Defining and measuring housing affordability – an alternative approach*,
http://www.nationwidefoundation.org.uk/wp-content/uploads/2019/06/Definingandmeasuringhousingaffordability.pdf
Last visited 24.2.20

Alfred, Dave (Ed.) (1988) *Robert Tressell lectures, 1981-88* (Workers Educational Association)

Ashton, Philip (16th November, 2018)
Statement on Visit to the United Kingdom, by Professor Philip Alston, United Nations Special Rapporteur on extreme poverty and human rights
https://www.ohchr.org/Documents/Issues/Poverty/EOM_GB_16Nov2018.pdf
Last visited 24.2.20

Barr, B. Loopstra, R. Reeves, M. Stuckler, D. Taylor-Robinson, D. Whitehead, M (2015)
First, do no harm': are disability assessments associated with adverse trends in mental health? In <u>Journal of Epidemiology and Community Health</u>, Volume 70, Issue 4
https://jech.bmj.com/content/70/4/339.full
Last visited 24.2.20

Bate, Alex, Bellis, Alexander and Philip Loft (22nd January, 2020) *The Troubled Families Programme (England)*, Briefing Paper Number 07585
https://researchbriefings.parliament.uk/ResearchBriefing/Summary/CBP-7585#fullreport
Last visited 24.2.20

Benn, Tony (1986) *Tressell the Teacher* in <u>Robert Tressell lectures</u>, *1981-88* (Workers Educational Association)

British Vehicle Rental and Leasing Association, *2019 Annual Review*,
https://www.bvrla.co.uk/uploads/assets/6e57986d-1944-46b6-bbe5bb90ccd56e2c/Annual-Review-2019Complete.pdf
Last visited 24.2.20

Brown, Gordon (25th November, 1997)
Pre-Budget Statement,
https://publications.parliament.uk/pa/cm199798/cmhansrd/vo971125/debtext/71125-06.htm
Last visited 24.2.20

Charity Commission, *Charities in England and Wales – 30 September 2018*
http://apps.charitycommission.gov.uk/ShowCharity/RegisterOfCharities/SectorData/SectorOverview.aspx
Last visited 24.2.20

Chartered Institute of Personnel and Development (August, 2019) *Executive pay in the FTSE 100 - 2019 review Is everyone getting a fair slice of the cake?*
https://www.cipd.co.uk/Images/ftse-100-executive-pay-report-2019_tcm18-62886.pdf
Last visited 24.2.20

Child Poverty Action Group, *The Causes of Poverty*,
https://cpag.org.uk/child-poverty/causes-poverty
Last visited 24.2.20

Chomsky, Noam (2003) *Understanding Power* (Vintage)

Coalition for Reform in Political Advertising (December, 2019) *Illegal, Indecent, Dishonest & Untruthful: How Political Advertising in the 2019 General Election Let us down.*
https://reformpoliticaladvertising.org/wp-content/uploads/2019/12/Illegal-Indecent-Dishonest-and-Untruthful-The-Coalition-for-Reform-in-Political-Advertising.pdf
Last visited 24.2.20

Cominetti, Nye (November, 2019) *Calculating a Living Wage for London and the rest of the UK*, Resolution Foundation Briefing,
https://www.livingwage.org.uk/sites/default/files/Living-wage-calculation-2019-20.pdf
Last visited 24.2.20

Connolly, Rachel (11th December, 2019) *From "broadband communism" to a "Marxist dystopia": how Labour's social democratic reforms have been branded as hard left fantasies*
https://www.prospectmagazine.co.uk/politics/from-broadband-communism-to-a-marxist-dystopia-how-labours-social-democratic-reforms-have-been-branded-as-hard-left-fantasies
Last visited 24.2.20

Department for Business, Energy & Industrial Strategy (30th May, 2019) *Trade Union Membership: Statistical Bulletin*
https://assets.publishing.service.gov.uk/government/uploads/system/uploads/attachment_data/file/805268/trade-union-membership-2018-statistical-bulletin.pdf
Last visited 24.2.20

Department for Work and Pensions (6th November, 2013) *Benefit sanctions – ending the 'something for nothing' culture*, Press Release.
https://www.gov.uk/government/news/benefit-

sanctions-ending-the-something-for-nothing-culture
Last visited 24.2.20

Farage, Nigel (2013) *Speech to UKIP Conference*, http://www.ukpol.co.uk/nigel-farage-2013-speech-to-ukip-conference/
Last visited 24.2.20

Fell, Matthew, (15th November, 2019) *CBI says Labour's plan "is not the way" to improve broadband*, https://www.theguardian.com/business/live/2019/nov/15/bt-claims-labour-nationalisation-plan-cost-100bn-business-live?page
Last visited 24.2.20

Financial Conduct Authority, (15th May, 2019) *Consumer credit — high-cost short-term credit lending data* https://www.fca.org.uk/data/consumer-credit-high-cost-short-term-credit-lending-data-jan-2019
Last visited 24.2.20

Financial Times (21st November, 2019) Labour's manifesto adds up to a recipe for decline, https://www.ft.com/content/1b35a81e-0c5f-11ea-b2d6-9bf4d1957a67
Last visited 24.2.20

Gerard, Liz (8th March, 2017) *Anti-immigration rhetoric: the poisonous xenophobia of our press*, article published in The New European, https://www.theneweuropean.co.uk/top-

stories/anti-immigration-rhetoric-the-poisonous-xenophobia-of-our-press-1-4921622
Last visited 24.2.20

Gosling, Tony, (6th June, 2019) *The Uk's 50 Biggest Landowners Revealed* – Lovemoney.com, posted on This Land is Ours website, http://tlio.org.uk/the-uks-50-biggest-landowners-revealed-lovemoney-com/
Last visited 24.2.20

HM Treasury, (2000) *Tackling Poverty and Making Work Pay – Tax Credits for the 21st Century*, https://revenuebenefits.org.uk/pdf/tax_cedits_for_the_21st_century.pdf
Last visited 24.2.20

Institute for Fiscal Studies (June, 2019)
Living standards, poverty and inequality in the UK: 2019
https://www.ifs.org.uk/uploads/R157-Living-Standards-Poverty-and-Inequality-2019.pdf
Last visited 24.2.20

International Monetary Fund (October, 2019)
World Economic Outlook: Global Manufacturing Downturn, Rising Trade Barriers
https://www.imf.org/en/Publications/WEO/Issues/2019/10/01/world-economic-outlook-october-2019
Last visited 24.2.20

Ipsos MORI (December, 2019)
How the voters voted in the 2019 election,
https://www.ipsos.com/sites/default/files/ct/news/documents/2019-12/general-election-2019-poll-aggregate-v8.pdf
Last visited 24.2.20

Jones, Jack (1984) *Robert Tressell's Message for Today*, in Robert Tressell lectures, *1981-88*, Workers Educational Association.

Joseph Rowntree Foundation (4th December, 2018) *UK Poverty 2018: A comprehensive analysis of poverty trends and figures*
https://www.jrf.org.uk/report/uk-poverty-2018
Last visited 24.2.20

Laughlin, Andrew, (1st June, 2018) *Which? investigation reveals 'staggering' level of smart home surveillance*, Which? Magazine, https://www.which.co.uk/news/2018/06/which-investigation-reveals-staggering-level-of-smart-home-surveillance/
Last visited 24.2.20

Liberty (2019) *A Guide to the Hostile Environment*, https://www.libertyhumanrights.org.uk/sites/default/files/Hostile%20Environment%20Guide%20%E2%80%93%20update%20May%202019_0.pdf
Last visited 24.2.20

Low Pay Commission (January, 2020)
National Minimum Wage, Report 2019,
https://assets.publishing.service.gov.uk/governm

ent/uploads/system/uploads/attachment_data/file/856590/LPC_Report_2019.pdf
Last visited 24.2.20

Mason, Paul (2016) *Postcapitalism: A Guide to Our Future*, London: Penguin.

Media Reform Coalition (2019)
Who Owns the UK Media?
https://www.mediareform.org.uk/wp-content/uploads/2019/03/FINALonline2.pdf
Last visited 24.2.20

Minford, Patrick (2019)
In One Bound We Can Be Free,
Economists for Free Trade,
https://www.economistsforfreetrade.com/wp-content/uploads/2019/01/In-One-Bound-We-Can-Be-Free-Upload-2.pdf
Last visited 24.2.20

Montacute, Rebecca, (January, 2018)
Internships -Unpaid, unadvertised, unfair,
https://www.suttontrust.com/wp-content/uploads/2018/01/Internships-2018-briefing.pdf
Last visited 24.2.20

National Audit Office (6th February, 2020)
Information held by the Department for Work & Pensions on deaths by suicide of benefit claimants
https://www.nao.org.uk/wp-content/uploads/2020/02/Information-held-by-the-DWP-on-

deaths-by-suicide-of-benefit-claimants.pdf
Last visited 24.2.20

Oborne, Peter, (2019) *The lies, falsehoods and misrepresentations of Boris Johnson and his government.*
https://boris-johnson-lies.com/
Last visited 24.2.20

Ofcom (17th May, 2018) *Pricing trends for communications services in the UK,*
https://www.ofcom.org.uk/__data/assets/pdf_file/0030/113898/pricing-report-2018.pdf
Last visited 24.2.20

Ofcom (4th July, 2019) *Communications Market Report 2019,*
https://www.ofcom.org.uk/__data/assets/pdf_file/0020/117065/communications-market-report-2019.pdf
Last visited 24.2.20

Office of National Statistics, (10th September, 2018) *EMP04: Employment by occupation*
https://www.ons.gov.uk/employmentandlabourmarket/peopleinwork/employmentandemployeetypes/datasets/employmentbyoccupationemp04
Last visited 24.2.20

Office of National Statistics, (25th March, 2019) *Which occupations are at highest risk of being automated?*
https://www.ons.gov.uk/employmentandlabourm

arket/peopleinwork/employmentandemployeetypes/articles/whichoccupationsareathighestriskofbeingautomated/2019-03-25
Last visited 24.2.20

Office for National Statistics (1st October, 2019) *Deaths of homeless people in England and Wales: 2018*
https://www.ons.gov.uk/peoplepopulationandcommunity/birthsdeathsandmarriages/deaths/bulletins/deathsofhomelesspeopleinenglandandwales/2018
Last visited 24.2.20

Office for National Statistics, (5th December, 2019) *Household debt in Great Britain April 2016 to March 2018,*
https://www.ons.gov.uk/peoplepopulationandcommunity/personalandhouseholdfinances/incomeandwealth/bulletins/householddebtingreatbritain/april2016tomarch2018
Last visited 24.2.20

Office of the Scottish Charity Regulator, *Charity Register Download,*
https://www.oscr.org.uk/about-charities/search-the-register/charity-register-download
Last visited 24.2.20

Oxford Economics, (June, 2019) *How robots change the world: What automation really means for jobs and productivity*

http://resources.oxfordeconomics.com/how-robots-change-the-world?source=recent-releases
Last visited 24.2.20

Samaritans (2017)
Dying from Inequality: Socioeconomic disadvantage and suicidal behaviour
https://media.samaritans.org/documents/Samaritans_Dying_from_inequality_report_-_summary.pdf
Last visited 24.2.20

Shelter, (17th December) *This is England: A picture of homelessness in 2019*,
https://england.shelter.org.uk/__data/assets/pdf_file/0009/1883817/This_is_England_A_picture_of_homelessness_in_2019.pdf
Last visited 24.2.20

Smee, Jess (4th December, 2019) *The rising clout of digital media and the UK election*, Article published on Euractiv.com.
https://www.euractiv.com/section/digital/opinion/the-rising-clout-of-digital-media-and-the-uk-election
Last visited 24.2.20

Tressell, Robert,
The Ragged Trousered Philanthropists, available free at:
http://www.gutenberg.org/ebooks/3608
Last visited 24.2.20

Tyler, Gloria (30th January, 2020) *Foodbanks in the UK*, Briefing Paper Number 8585, https://researchbriefings.parliament.uk/Research Briefing/Summary/CBP-8585#fullreport
Last visited 24.2.20

Welfare Reform and Work Act 2016
http://www.legislation.gov.uk/ukpga/2016/7/contents/enacted/data.htm
Last visited 24.2.20

Willis, Norman (1982) *Robert Tressell and the Trade Unions in the 1980s* in <u>Robert Tressell lectures</u>, *1981-88*, Workers Educational Association.

World Trade Organization, *Agreement on Agriculture*, https://www.wto.org/english/docs_e/legal_e/14-ag_01_e.htm
Last visited 24.2.20

Wren-Lewis, Simon (2018) *Labour's Fiscal Credibility Rule in Context*, in <u>Economics for the Many</u>, John McDonnel (Ed.) (Verso)

Zuboff, Shoshana (2019) The Age of Surveillance Capitalism (Profile Books)

On Tressell and his book

Ball, F. C. (1973) *One of the Damned: The Life and Times of Robert Tressell* (Lawrence & Wishart)

Harker, Dave (2003) *Tressell: The Real Story of The Ragged Trousered Philanthropists* (Zed)

Hernon, Ian (2015) *Robert Tressell - A Life in Hell: The Biography of the Author and His Ragged Trousered Philanthropists* (Red Axe Books)

Hyslop, Jonathan (2001) *A Ragged Trousered Philanthropist and the Empire: Robert Tressell in South Africa*, History Workshop Journal, No. 51, pp. 64-86

Mitchell, Jack (1969) *Robert Tressell and The Ragged Trousered Philanthropists*, (Lawrence & Wishart)

Ó Donghaile, Deaglán (2018) *Modernism, class and colonialism in Robert Noonan's The Ragged Trousered Philanthropists*, Irish Studies Review, 26:3, 374-389

TUC Collections, University of North London, handwritten manuscript.
http://www.unionhistory.info/ragged/browse.php?Where=irn+%3D+4001756+
Last visited 24.2.20

Young, James D. (1985) Militancy, *English Socialism and the Ragged Trousered Philanthropists*, Journal of Contemporary History, Vol. 20, No. 2, Working-Class and Left-Wing Politics, pp. 283-303

About the Author

Dave Lowes is an independent scholar and a member of Unite's CASA Community branch, Liverpool University UCU Branch and the IWW. He also attends Liverpool's Socialist Theory Study Group and subscribes to North West Labour History, and the Socialist History Society.

Previous monographs include:

Cuts, Privatisation and Resistance (Merlin Press, 2012)

The Anti-Capitalist Dictionary (Zed Books, 2006)

Printed in Great Britain
by Amazon